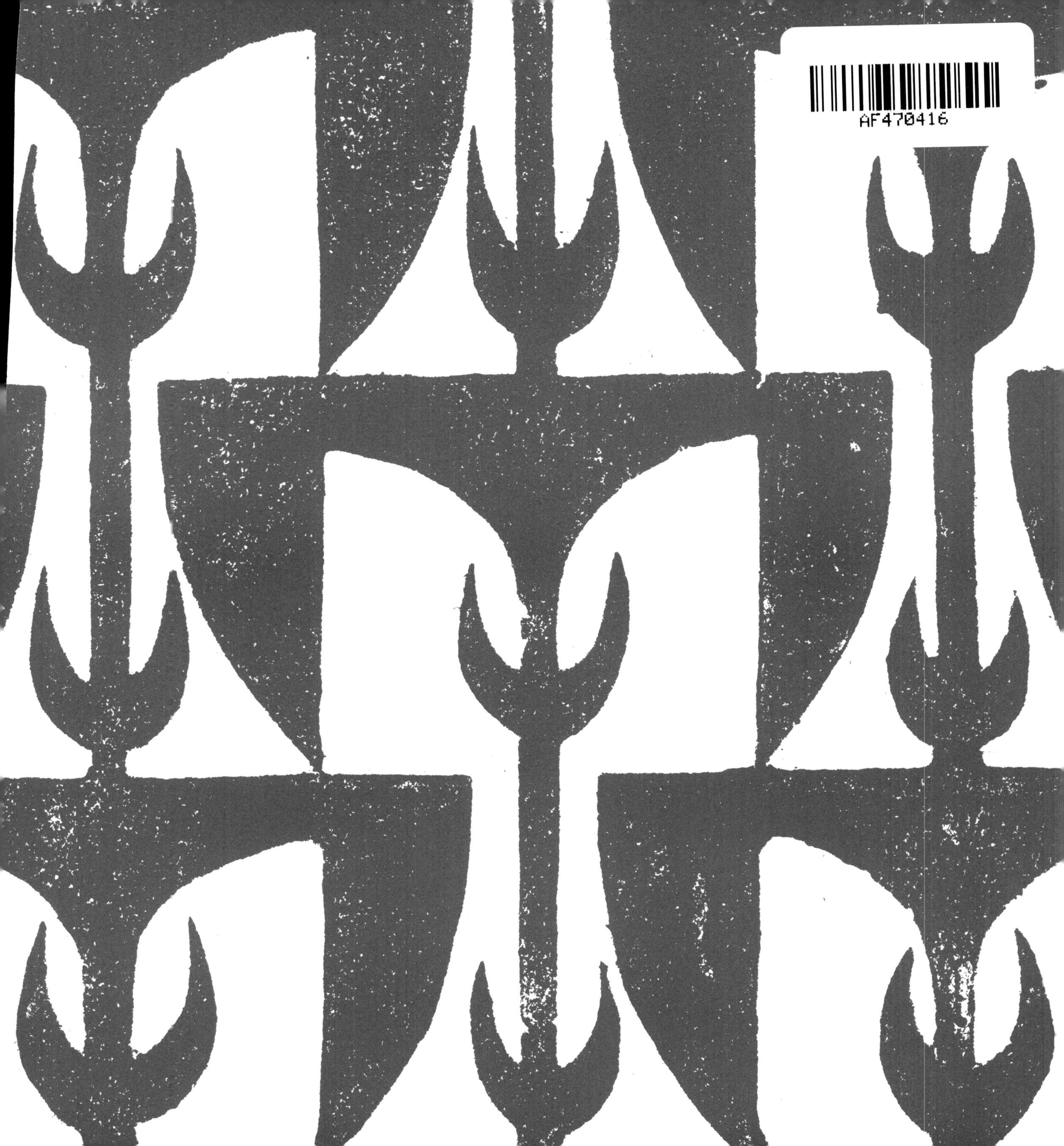

GEORGE KENNETH SON SCULPTURE

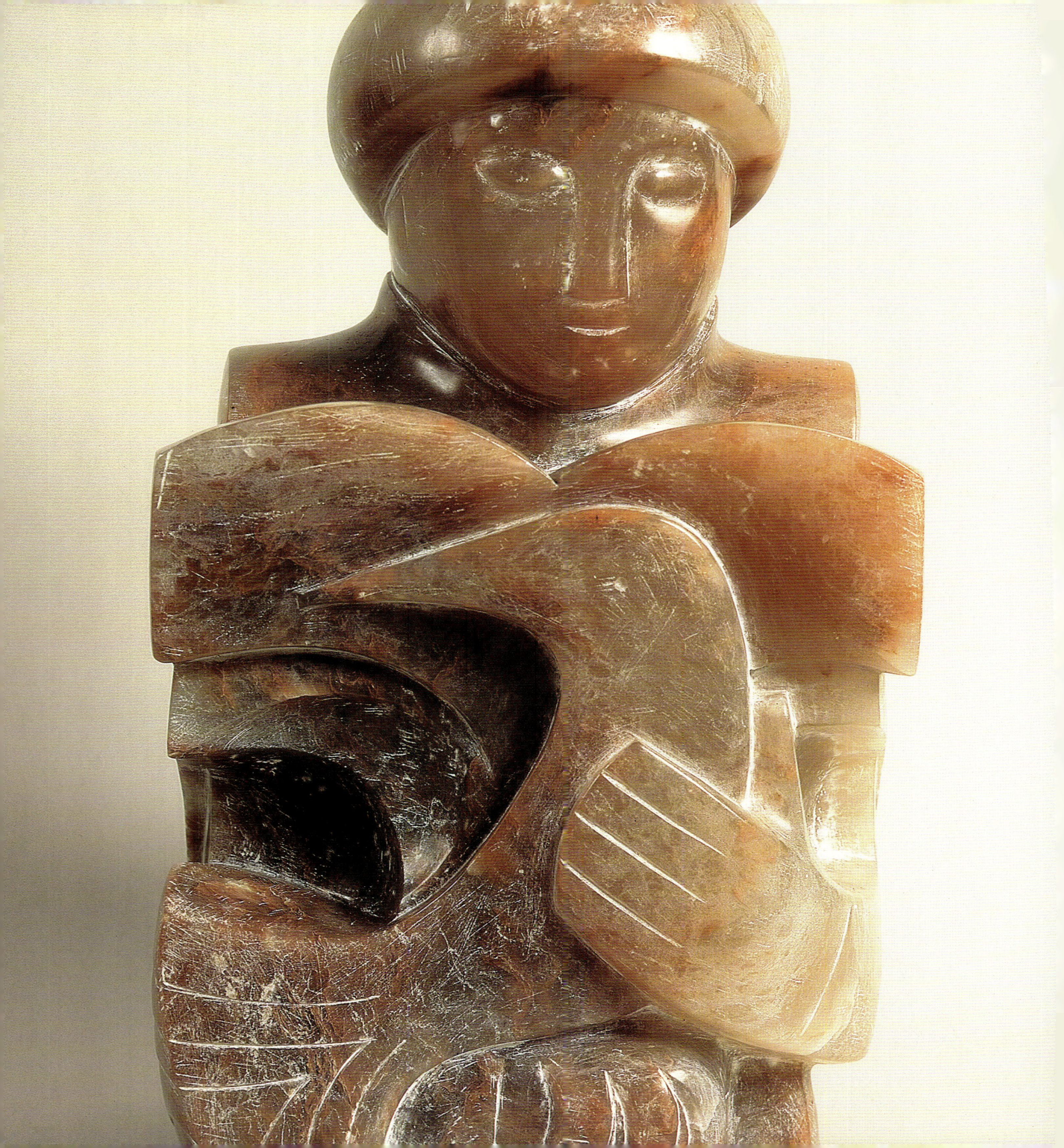

Simon Hucker

GEORGE KENNETHSON

A Modernist Rediscovered

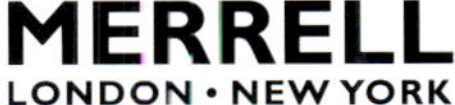

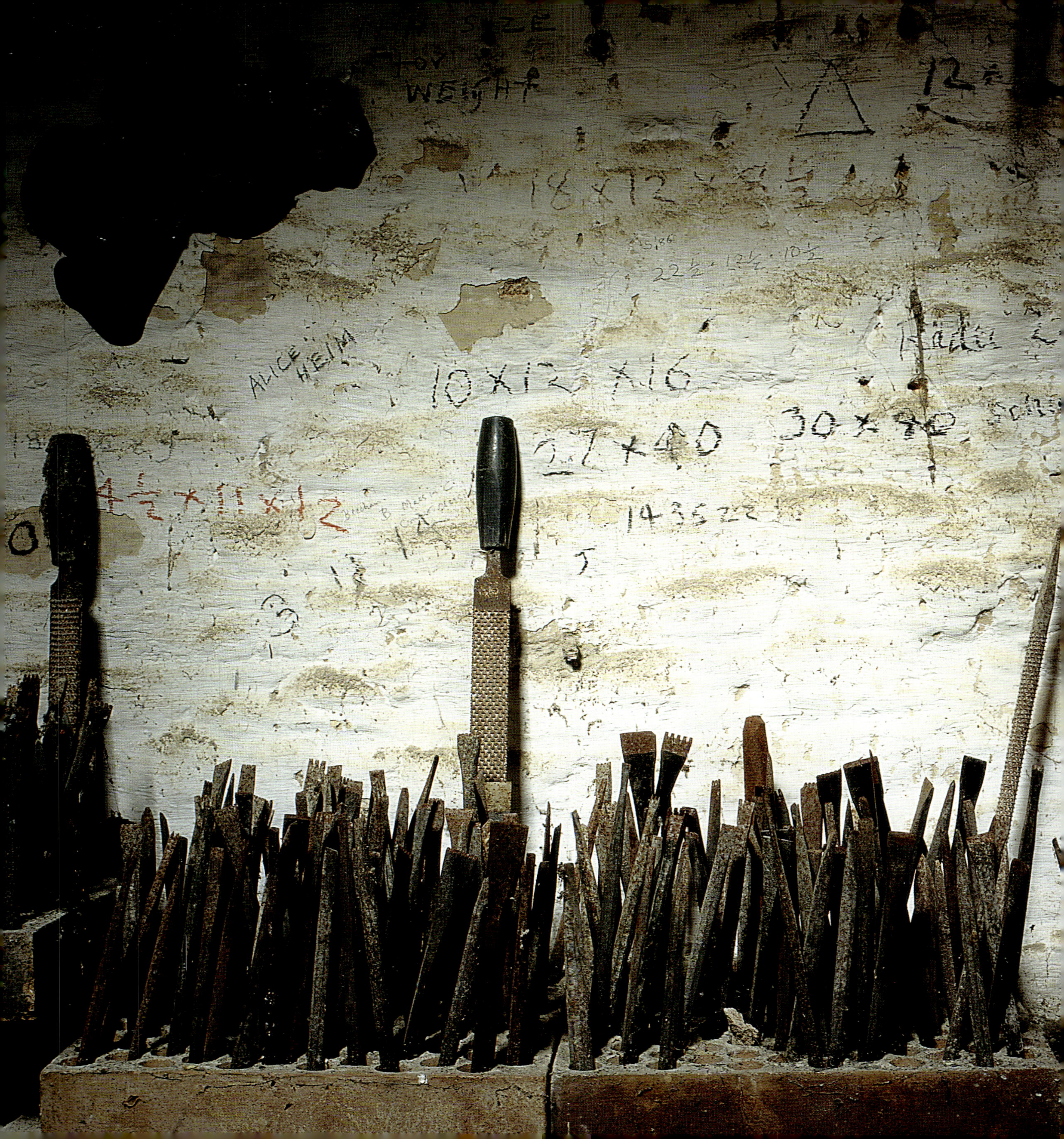
WEIGHT
ALICE HEIM
10X12 X16
27×40
4½×11×12

CONTENTS

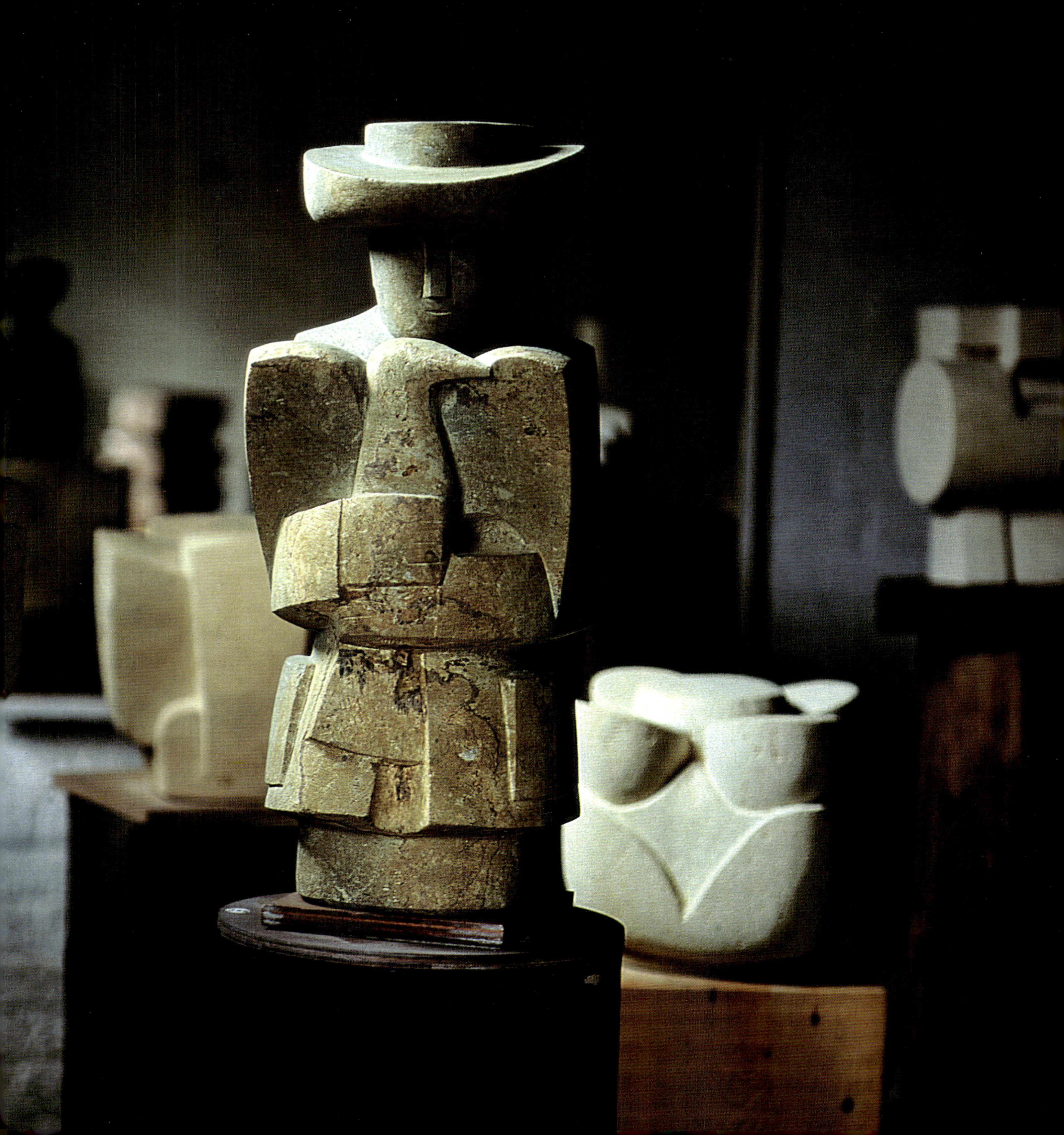

FOREWORD

Studio interior: *Man Holding a Bird*, 1960s

1910 was not the best year to be born a sculptor. It is remarkable how twentieth-century British sculpture came in distinct waves, each apparently overtaking and eclipsing the one before. The arrival of Britart at Damien Hirst's *Freeze* exhibition in 1988 is still fresh in the memory, whether we saw the show or not.[1] But starting at the beginning, we find Jacob Epstein, Eric Gill and Frank Dobson born in 1880, 1882 and 1886; Henry Moore and Barbara Hepworth in 1898 and 1903. The third wave – Reg Butler, Lynn Chadwick, Bernard Meadows, Kenneth Armitage and Robert Adams (the Fifties generation) – followed each other, year by year, from 1913 to 1917. And the Sixties revolution was heralded by Anthony Caro, born in 1924, with his 'New Generation' of students from St Martin's School of Art born between 1934 and 1937.

Between two waves, and regardless of what this meant in terms of the sculpture itself, George Kennethson missed out on the hype. He was twenty-nine at the outbreak of war, which he spent as a committed pacifist in rural Oxfordshire, and for the last forty years of his life he was even further off the beaten track, in Oundle in Northamptonshire.

As Kennethson felt his way from painting towards sculpture in the late 1930s, Moore and Hepworth were inevitable role models, with Dobson, Gill and Epstein in the not-too-distant background, all with their shared commitment to 'truth to materials'. The way ahead for Kennethson was clear, and certainly his early sculptures show that Moore and Dobson were within his sights. When the next generations moved into bronze, welded steel and synthetics, and even Moore and Hepworth extended into plaster and bronze, Kennethson resolutely picked up and carried the torch for 'direct carving' in stone. As the years went on it would become a lonelier journey, and in later life he would scour the London galleries for kindred spirits.

There is an obstinate streak running through Kennethson's life and work. While Moore explored the relationship of humankind to the natural landscape from which his materials derived, and Hepworth speculated on our place in the cosmos, Kennethson frequently concerned himself with a more everyday reality. His subjects were "the sea, birds, plants, the land, sky even and humanity, motifs common in the world of painting in which I was trained and in which I've always been deeply interested".[2] A woman pouring a glass of milk or water from a jug suggests a seventeenth-century Dutch painting rather than a stone carving, but the Cubists had introduced such objects into their sculptures and there is a modern and sculptural sense to it. Like Vermeer, Kennethson sensed the universal in the passing moment, and, in this context, his practice of photography – examples of which follow – is worth noting.

On a recent visit to Kennethson's studio to meet his wife, Eileen, and one of his five sons, we found ourselves grabbing his father's old, but still effective, binoculars to identify the source of a bird's song in a fir tree across the roofs. In Kennethson's lifetime that moment might well have found its way into sculptural form. Birds were a particular passion, and there is still a case of stuffed birds on the landing. In the sculptures they can barely be perceived – the mere suggestion of a wing or a neck – for here Kennethson veered towards the abstract, and it is the elusiveness of flight and song, the essence of the bird, that he attempted to encapsulate in stone.

It was one of these sculptures that first introduced me to Kennethson's work when I arrived in Cambridge in 1992. Jim Ede, the founder of Kettle's Yard, had set *Construction – Birds* low down against a window so that the afternoon light gives life to the translucent alabaster. On the table above is Henri Gaudier-Erzeska's *Dancer*, and across the room are two of Gaudier's early essays in direct carving. Downstairs, in a corner, beneath a skylight, is one of the most unlikely sculptures, another alabaster by Kennethson. Who, as a stone carver, would have dared to attempt the expanse and flux of the ocean's waves? Diagonally opposite is Gaudier's *Birds Erect* or *Rising Forms*, whose abstraction of nature's forces perhaps come closest as a bold precursor.

A little later I visited Kennethson in the old brewery in Oundle, where he had moved in 1959. Ironically for a stone carver in one of England's most stone-built towns, the house and brewery buildings are of red brick. We passed from building to building, where sea and birds mingled with figures and heads in a myriad variety of English stones. The sea, it turned out, was also derived from ordinary life, from annual holidays on the Isle of Purbeck in Dorset; it was a fascination to be tackled in dogged defiance of the acknowledged limitations of stone carving. And, despite the scale of theme, the sculptures of sea were of the same modest size as sculptures of workmen going about their business. Setting aside the easy option of monumentality, Kennethson was striving towards an abstract language, sometimes verging on the machine-like, that would encapsulate the inexorable forces and rhythms of the waves. There were no pretensions to grandeur or heroism, and characteristically he referred to his workroom rather than to his studio. For all his training at the Royal Academy Schools, to be an artist was to be a workman whose job was to make art.

Jim Ede had been one of the first to appreciate the qualities of George Kennethson's art, and through him countless visitors to Kettle's Yard have made their own discovery. Kennethson had written to Ede that "I keep reaching the edge of despair at being unable to show my work anywhere, let alone sell it".[3] but, in his later years and since, he found recognition through Madeleine Ponsonby and Rosanna Wilson Stephens at The New Art Centre in London and at Roche Court in Wiltshire, and now through exhibitions organized independently by Rosanna. It could be argued that Kennethson was born at the wrong time and lived in the wrong place. He felt out on the edge, but from there he pushed the tradition of stone carving, "a strikingly minority language",[4] in directions it had not been before.

Michael Harrison
Director
Kettle's Yard
Cambridge

Studio interior: *Standing Figure*, c. 1970, with exhibition posters for Kettle's Yard, Cambridge, behind

Overleaf
Studio interior with, on far left, *Coronation*, 1952–53 (see plate 1)

Notes

1 *Freeze* was organized by Damien Hirst in a disused London dock warehouse. It included work by several of his contemporaries at Goldsmiths, such as Tracey Emin, Sarah Lucas and Michael Landy.

2 Quoted in *Translations from Life and Nature: Stone Carvings 1950–1985*, exhib. cat., Peterborough Museum and Art Gallery, 1986.

3, 4 From letters to Jim Ede, Kettle's Yard Archive, Cambridge.

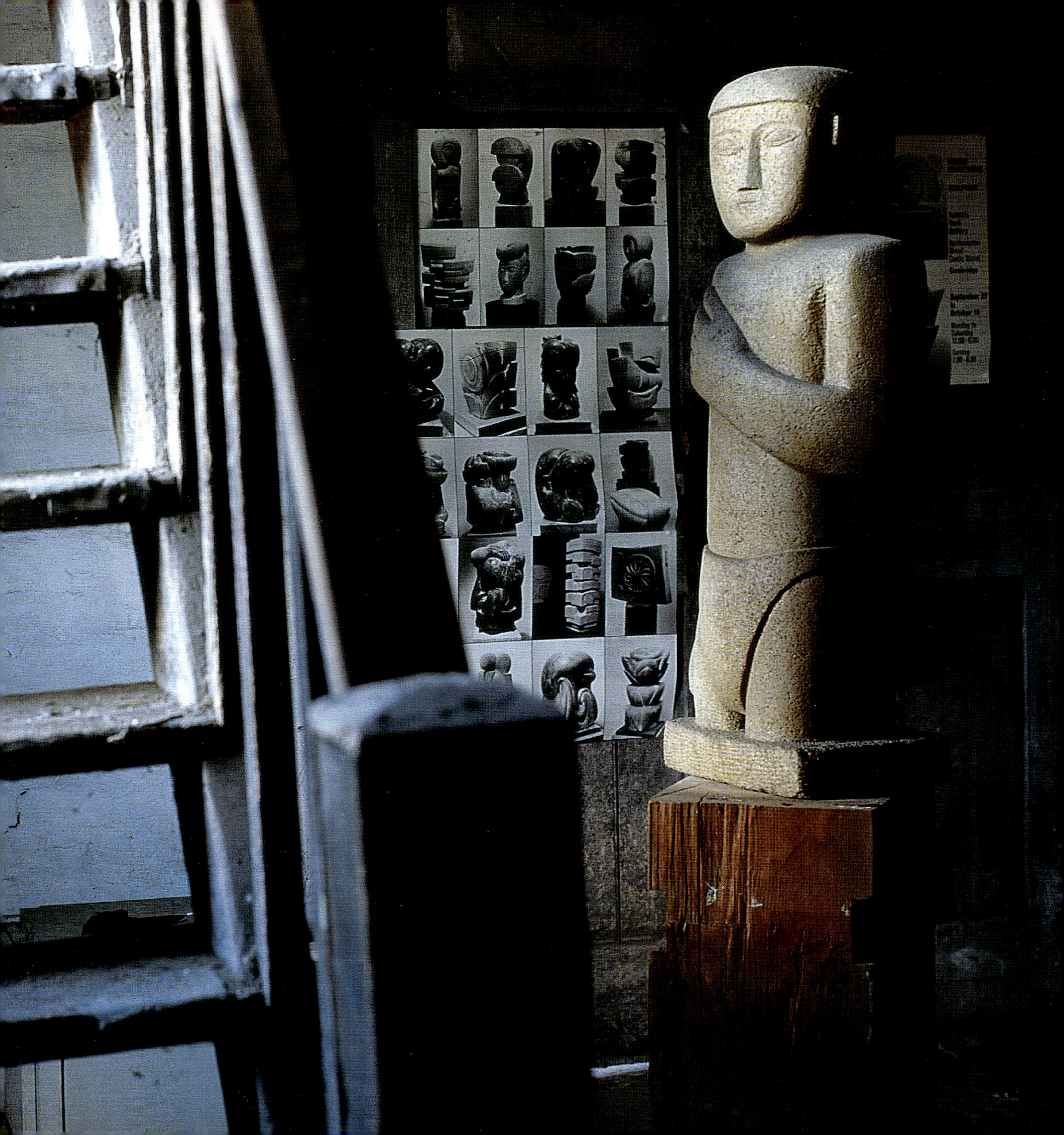

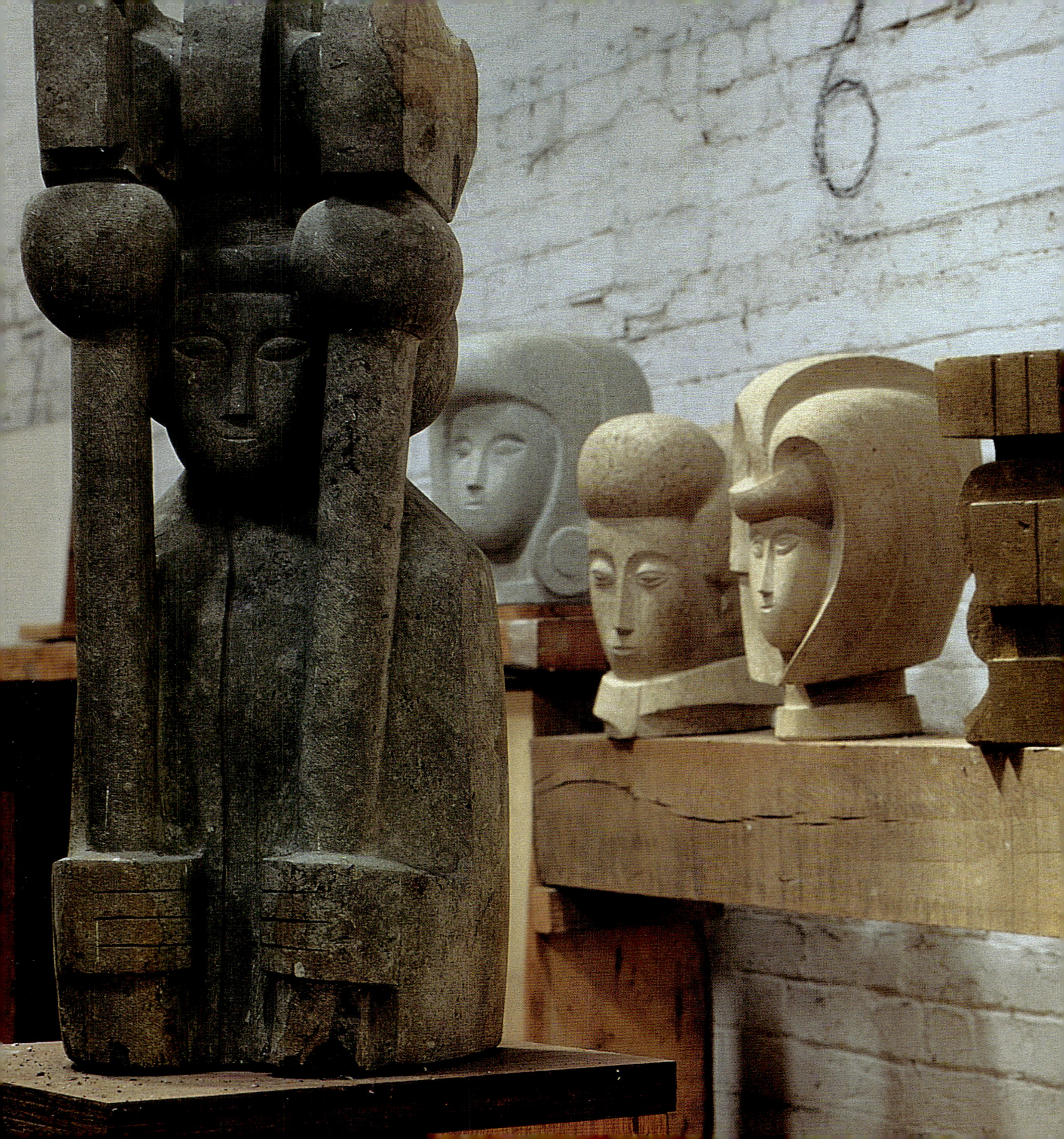

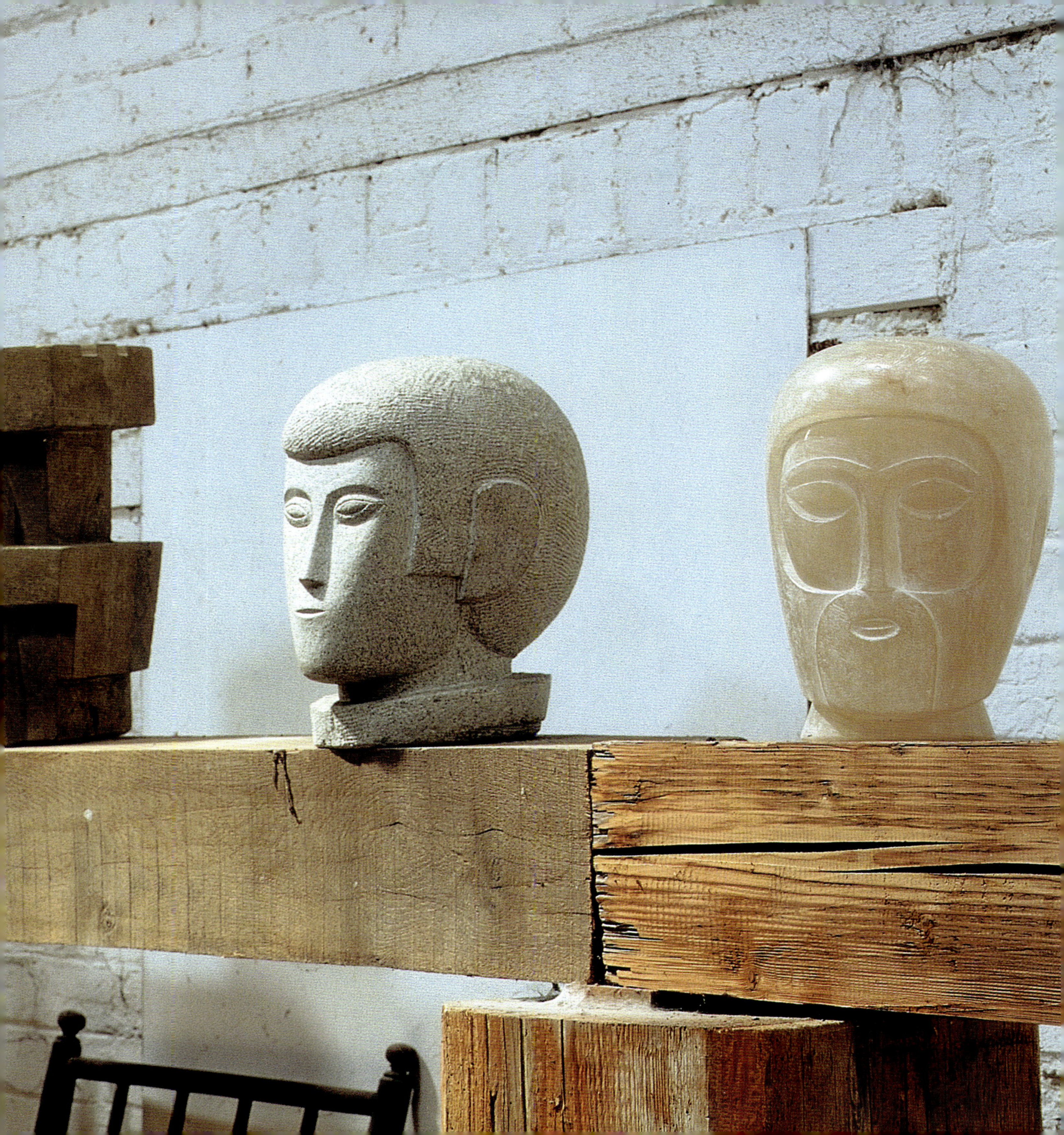

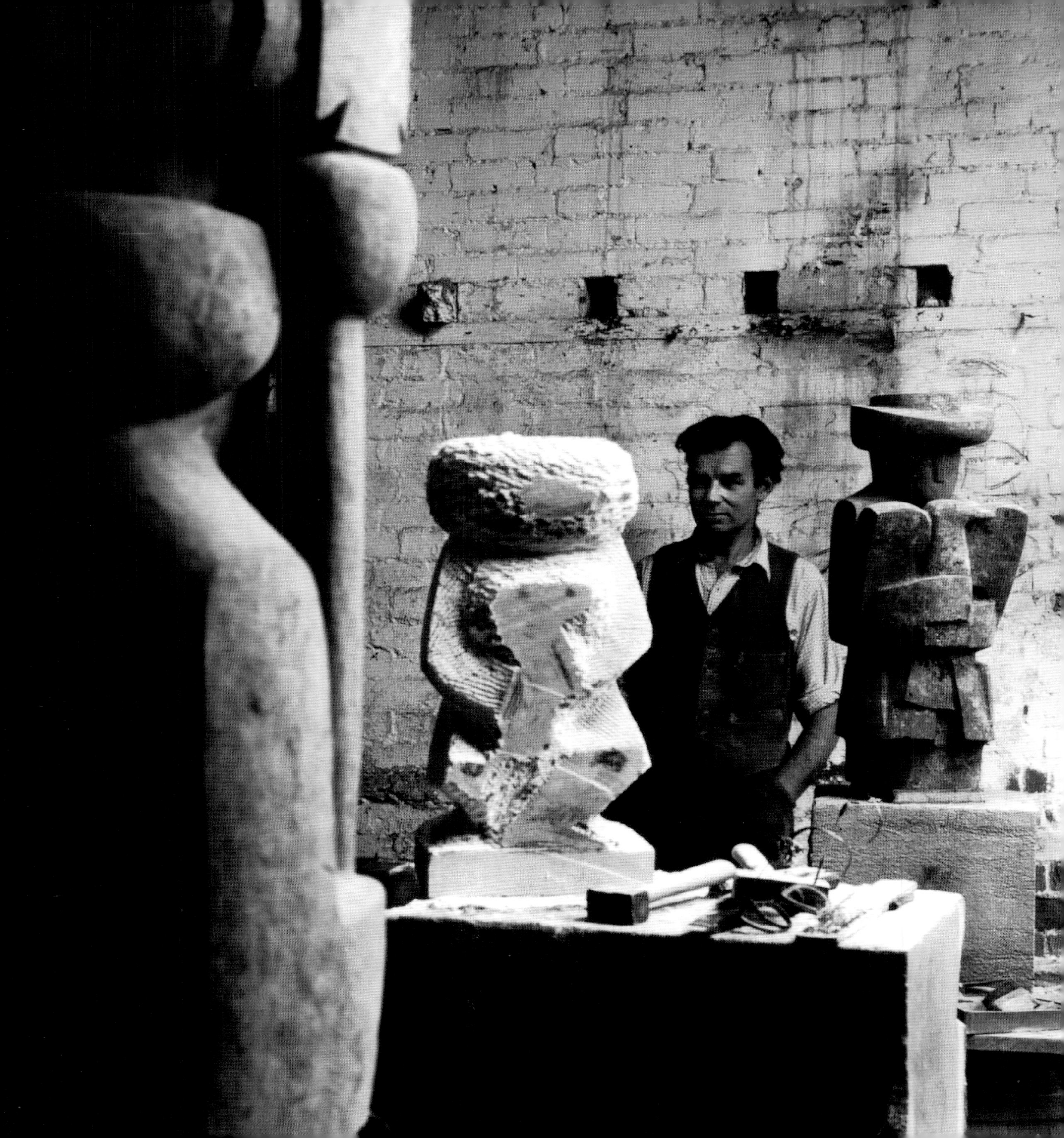

A MODERNIST REDISCOVERED

Fig. 1
Portrait of the sculptor in his studio with work in progress, 1953

In this particular medium, with its methods, limitations and language, I search for a new approach to the balancing act between the claims of abstract values and natural perceptions; translations from life and nature is how I see them – as systems of rhythmic and expressive relationships in space, to me a kind of fusion of music and architecture, rather delicately drawn out of each individual unique piece of material of a certain size, quality and nature.

George Kennethson

George Kennethson was born Arthur George Landseer Mackenzie in Richmond upon Thames, Surrey, in 1910. Although he remained Arthur to his friends and family throughout his life, he adopted the name George Kennethson as his professional identity in the early 1970s, Mackenzie being Scots for 'son of Kenneth'. The reason for this was simple: in his eyes, his work as a sculptor, to which he dedicated over five decades, represented a life in itself. His daily engagement with his material is what defined him as an artist, and so the genial and softly spoken Arthur Mackenzie was necessarily different from the man who relentlessly pursued his own unique vision, working for long periods in virtual isolation, at odds with prevailing fashions and movements.

George Kennethson was, in a way, someone who existed purely through his work and, specifically, through the process of carving in stone. Over the course of his life, Kennethson filled countless sketchbooks with drawings and notes, and yet it was during his physical encounter with blocks of limestone, alabaster, marble and granite that he really decided how the image would be resolved. His artistic journey was lived out, day after day, through the process of carving. As such, it took on the sense of being a parallel existence, complete with work, tiredness and pain, conducted against the slow passing of time. Works such as *Traveller* (plates 4 and 23), therefore, may be seen as partly autobiographical – as representations of the sculptor striking out along the path he chose for himself.

Kennethson's father was a Classics scholar and lawyer, and the young George grew up in a well-off and cultured environment. After the death of his mother, Beatrice, in 1920, he spent his holidays from boarding school (which he disliked) among artistic aunts and socialite uncles. Even as a child, though, Kennethson could not stand the thought of 'being like Uncle Edwin', who seemed to spend most of his life travelling. He did, however, get on well with one of his great uncles who spent his spare time designing boats and carving wooden boxes in intricate designs, suggesting an early love for making things with his hands that would eventually find expression in his life as a sculptor.

While still quite young, Kennethson decided that he wanted to become an artist, and, in 1927, aged seventeen, he attended the St John's Wood School of Art in London. He studied under Pat Millard, a renowned draughtsman, who would later become head of London's Goldsmiths College, from where he would play an important role in the setting up of polytechnics in the 1960s and 1970s. It was at St John's Wood that Kennethson began to sketch every day, something he would do throughout his life, and although his sculptures were defined principally by the structure of each block, all his works have clear, flowing lines running through them that owe much to a lifetime of drawing.

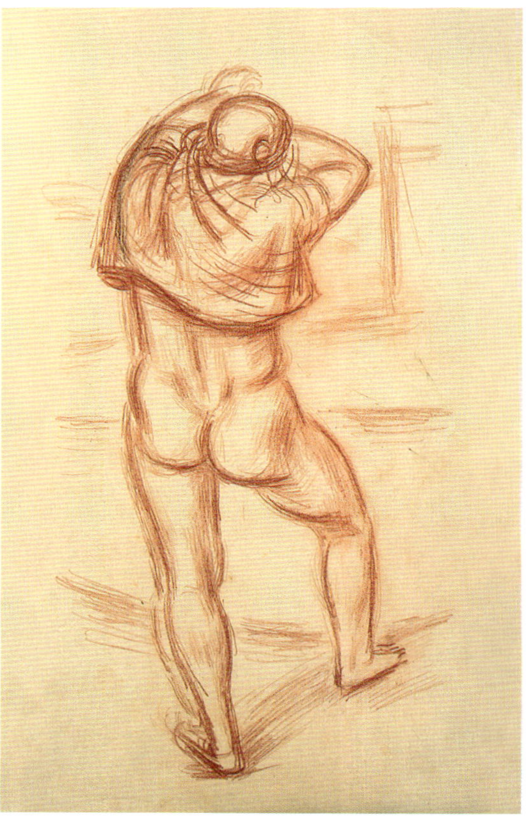

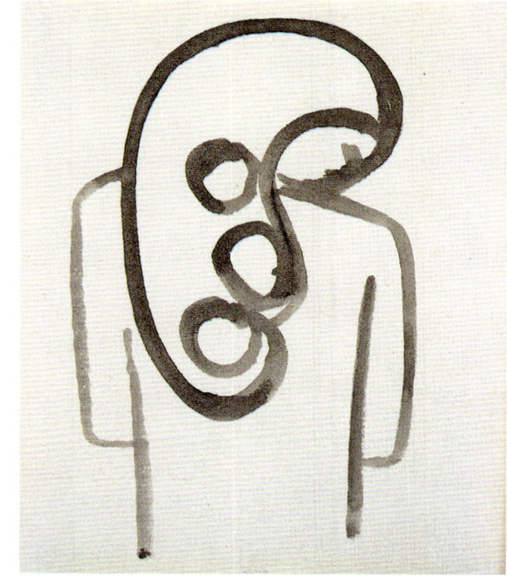

Fig. 2
Female Figure Undressing
c. 1930
Red Conté on paper
40 x 25 cm (15¾ x 9¾ in.)

Fig. 3
Girl's Back with Curled Hair
c. 1960
Ink and wash on paper
16.5 x 12 cm (6½ x 4¾ in.)

Kennethson's time at St John's Wood prepared him well for the Royal Academy Schools, which he entered in 1929 as a painting student. Drawing formed an essential part of the training at the academy, where the students still attended life-drawing classes and copied from plaster casts of Classical sculpture, as they had done since its inception in 1768. Rather than being given any formal teaching, the students were overseen by visiting academicians, such as Thomas Monnington, Walter Bayes, Ernest Jackson and Walter Russell. It was Russell who was most admired by the students, teaching them, in particular, how to convey form and structure to give solidity to drawing the human figure. Only a few of Kennethson's drawings survive from the period, showing him working in traditional 'Academic' style, with volume built up through intricate shading and cross-hatching. Indeed, there is nothing particularly 'sculptural' about them, except their evident interest in mass and weight, unlike his later drawings, which are done as if the pencil or brush were a chisel (figs. 2 and 3).

The second and third years at the Royal Academy Schools were also very traditional: painting and drawing from models in the life classes and making a copy of an Old Master painting from the National Gallery. Yet it was impossible for art students of Kennethson's generation (as it had been for the likes of Henry Moore and Barbara Hepworth a few years earlier) to ignore what was going on outside the college walls. London's commercial galleries were showing a wide selection of Post-Impressionist, Cubist and Surrealist art, and the writings of such early Modernists as Roger Fry and Herbert Read were starting to have an incendiary effect among avant-garde circles. As George's widow, Eileen, has commented, everyone at the time was looking towards Paris.

As a painter, Kennethson was deeply influenced by the work of Cézanne, in particular the way he *constructed* his still-lifes and landscapes from a simple vocabulary of basic, almost elemental geometric forms (sphere, cylinder and cube). Kennethson's decision to abandon painting for sculpture after he left college is perhaps less surprising, then, given that the painter he most admired did most to break down the illusionistic surface of figurative painting and assert the underlying physicality of the world of appearances and of painting itself.

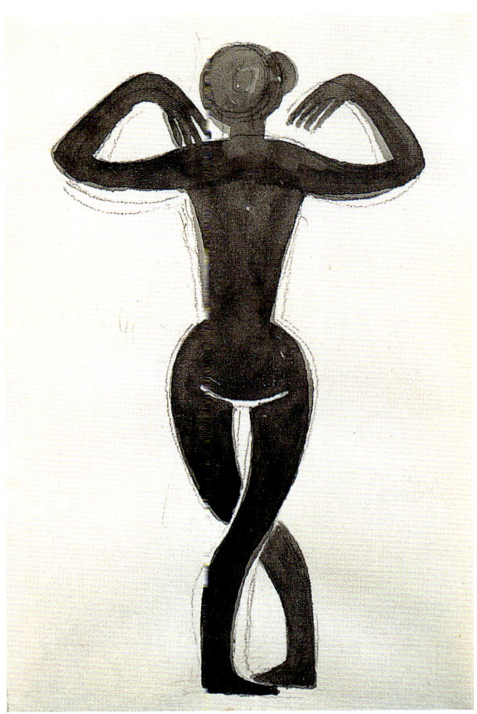

Fig. 4
Stylized Girl Dancing
c. 1960
Pencil and ink wash on paper
26 x 16 cm (10¼ x 6¼ in.)

A key influence on the development of Kennethson's later career was the range of exhibitions in London of so-called 'primitive' non-European art, especially tribal wood carvings from Africa and stone sculpture from India. Ever since artists had fallen under the spell of the masks and fetishes in the great ethnographic collections of Paris and Berlin at the end of the nineteenth century, the European avant-garde had looked towards 'primitive' art as a source of 'universal truth'. It was seen to represent a physical and spiritual 'reality' that had been lost under the refinements of the academic 'naturalism' that had dominated Western art since the Renaissance (regardless of the fact that this 'naturalism' was itself based on a highly schematic system from Ancient Greece). For someone such as Roger Fry, 'primitive' artists "without ever attaining anything like representational accuracy ... have complete freedom" (Roger Fry, *Vision and Design*). It was this freedom that was so prized by the European 'Modernist Primitivists'.

The new science of psychoanalysis, and the work of Jung in particular, was also very influential on the cultural appropriation of the 'primitive' into the 'modern', with Jung's ideas on universal psychological archetypes, common across all cultures, being translated into a theory of universal visual, formal archetypes. 'Primitive' art, seemingly unconcerned with 'naturalism', was seen to have bypassed imitation and gone straight to the truth.

Perhaps the most important idea of 'Modernist Primitivism' was that 'primitive' form was somehow intrinsically tied in with 'primitive' technique, which itself ignored the subtlety, variation and sophisticated processes of much non-European art. The tribal 'artist-maker' was also seen to be not aiming, Pygmalion-like, to transform the materials he was using, but complying with their inherent forms and shapes. Because of these ideas, sculptors abandoned modelling in plaster or clay (in preparation for casting in metal) to take up carving in wood or stone, which was seen as more directly expressive, less mediated. From this developed the concept of 'truth to materials': that material had inherent properties that should be used, rather than hidden. This idea can be seen as the beginning of the interest in process that is arguably fundamental to the development of sculpture in the twentieth century, from the 'Modernist Primitivism' of Constantin Brancusi, Ossip Zadkine or Jacob Epstein, to the use of industrial materials and fabrication techniques of such American Minimalists as Donald Judd, Robert Morris and Carl Andre.

For Kennethson, 'truth to materials' was an extremely important idea and much more than just a theory that happened to be in vogue when he was a student. His writings are suffused with it (fig. 5). He considered sculpture to be an "endless compromise between the medium and the idea ... . It's not so much the art of the possible as the art of the appropriate." He saw his process as "exploring with very inadequate maps", with "nothing [being] resolved as the stone always throws up new challenges and directions … . planes, rhythms and weights must be felt physically … . if there is anything of value it's from co-operation not destruction." Significantly, one of his favourite works was a figure of a circus tightrope walker, which he felt was a perfect metaphor for the balancing act he undertook each time he took a chisel to a block of stone.

In Kennethson's final year at the Royal Academy he met Eileen Guthrie, whom he married in 1938. Eileen was a first-year painting student and her first impressions were of an energetic and impressively built man, with a mischievous and rather off-beat sense of humour, who seemed dedicated to being an artist and who, by this time, was already thinking about becoming a sculptor. In common with many of their milieu, George and Eileen were left wing in their politics and interested in all things avant-garde: art, architecture, photography, music, film and theatre. As well as going on painting trips together in Cornwall and the north of England with fellow students, they also travelled to Paris, where George tracked down the work of Aristide Maillol, Zadkine and Brancusi. A few years later they returned to Paris to see Pablo Picasso's recently finished *Guernica* (1937), which moved them profoundly, both artistically and politically.

As an aspiring sculptor in London, Kennethson could not help but be influenced by the work of the rising stars of British sculpture, Barbara Hepworth, John Skeaping and Henry Moore. At a certain point in the 1920s the work of these three artists, living and working together at the Mall Studios in Hampstead, north London, became almost interchangeable. Somewhat ironically, however, this similarity also made their work distinctive as a new and coherent 'brand' of English Modernism.

One of Kennethson's earliest surviving sculptures, *Mother and Child* (plate 2), clearly shows the influence of Moore, Hepworth and Skeaping's works of the 1920s: the frontal, totemic pose; the geometric body slightly rounded off, but kept raw at the hands and the child's feet; and the overall

To seek harmony: to give life.
To educate myself.
Above all, it's to do with relationships.
Research & experiment, a battle for harmony.
Memory: What is the residue?
The price is continuous dissatisfaction.
Relationship of the planes, and their junctions.
A harmony of planes & masses.
I don't believe in wanton destruction. I am totally against it.

Fig. 5
A 'jotting', one of the sculptor's notes to himself to record his ideas and working practice

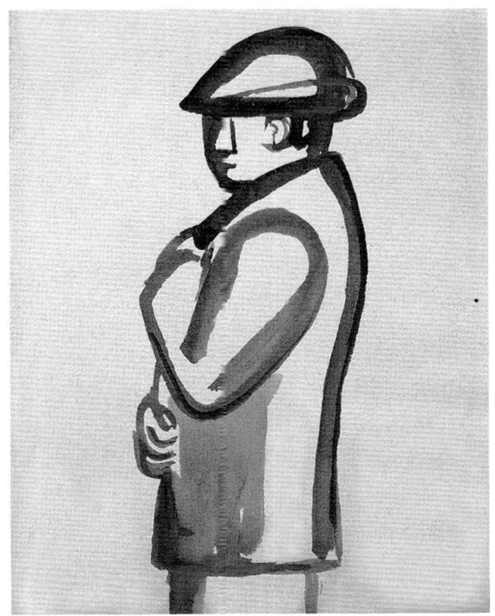

Fig. 6
Standing Man in Cap
c. 1960
Ink and wash on blue paper
19.5 x 14 cm ($7\frac{3}{4}$ x $5\frac{1}{2}$ in.)

sense of bulk and weight. Even in this early work, however, there are elements that are pure Kennethson: the asymmetrical outline when viewed from the front; square-cut hollows and overhangs whose sharpness and precision reassert the work's origin as a sawn block of stone; the eyes left blank, with the face articulated by the simplest of means – elegant curved brows and a broad, angular nose.

After leaving college, Kennethson took a studio in St John's Wood, where at first he continued to paint. Around 1936, however, he began to make terracotta models, which he considered to be 'three-dimensional sketches' for future stone carvings. Meanwhile, to gain the skills he would require, Kennethson began helping out at a sculptor's works in Chelsea, west London. In 1938 George and Eileen moved to Uffington in Oxfordshire, to a house overlooked by the Iron Age white horse etched into the chalk of the hills, which must have been an inspiration to the young sculptor. Here, at last, Kennethson had the room he needed to sculpt in earnest, as well as a wide and open landscape in which he could walk and think.

Kennethson was a committed pacifist and, despite being passed by a medical commission as being borderline fit for duty, he had to face two military tribunals before being exempted from active service in World War II. The village, knowing that George and Eileen were artists, half expected them to be different anyway and so George's pacifism never became a matter of contention. Instead, the family took in evacuees from London and the occasional refugee from Europe.

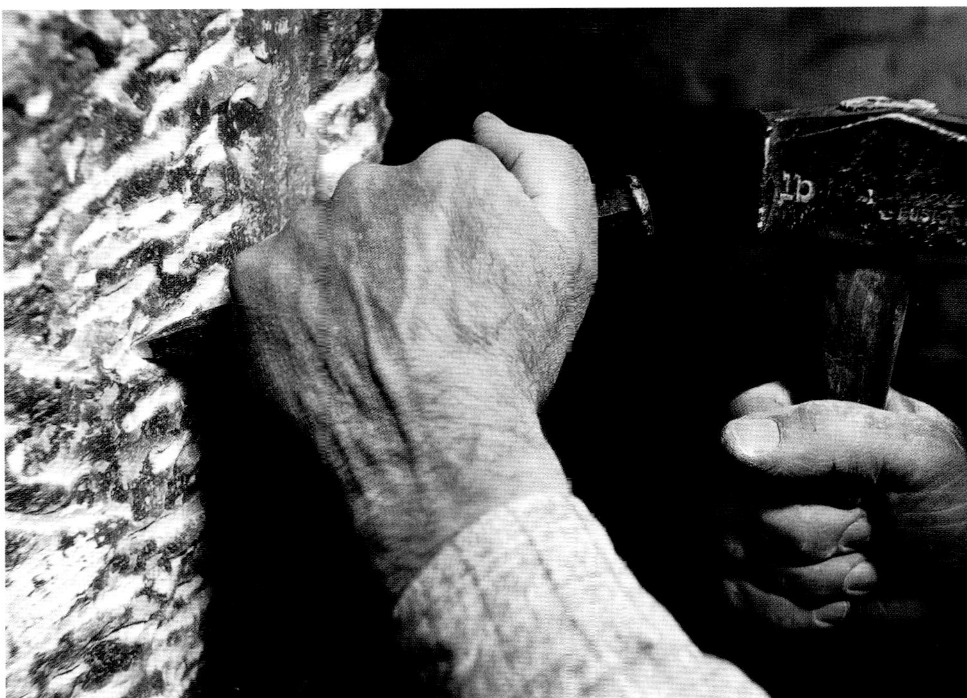

Fig. 7
The sculptor at work with chisel and hammer, *c.* 1980

Uffington's various characters became the source of ideas and inspiration for the young sculptor. One day, he saw one of the local villagers through his studio window, carrying a rolled-up straw mattress to the blacksmith's forge down the road. This chance encounter inspired the *Man with a Mattress* sculptures that he made throughout his career (fig. 8). These works are, in part, about formal contrasts, between the cylinder of the mattress, the sphere of the head (often tilted at angles under the weight) and the vertical lines of the forearms. Yet they are also about the symbolism of burdens, a secular St Christopher, where the underlying value is labour.

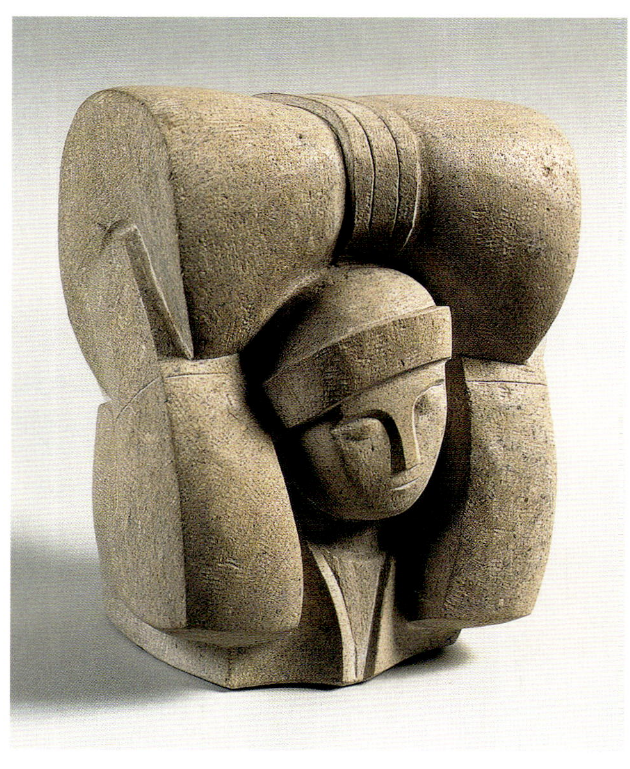

Fig. 8
Man with a Mattress
Date unknown
Clipsham stone
40.5 x 30.5 x 21.5 cm (16 x 12 x 8½ in.)
Estate of the artist: reserve collection

The inspiration for the *Traveller* series (plates 4 and 23) can also be seen to date from this period. Petrol rationing and the requisitioning of private cars by the government meant that everyday life in Uffington had something of the atmosphere of a book by Thomas Hardy, one of Kennethson's favourite authors. Everybody walked and loads were carried on shoulders or on handcarts. These figures are always kitted out in a very practical manner, with wide-brimmed hats, haversacks and deep pockets. They are the itinerant workers whose footsteps scored paths across the English landscape in the centuries before the Industrial Revolution, men whose lives were defined by their skills, by their hands. At the same time, Uffington was full of evacuees from the Blitz and so these pieces have a darker side: journey becomes displacement and the invisible wind against which these figures seem to brace themselves blows as much from history as it does from the landscape. Towards the end of his life Kennethson made two works – mothers sheltering children in their arms – entitled *Refugees* in direct response to the persecution of the Kurds in northern Iraq by the country's president, Saddam Hussein. His concern for the tragic consequences of war remained undiminished.

After the War Kennethson began to work on three monumental sculptures: two standing figures, including a mother and child, and a figure of a fallen medieval knight, which was turned into a memorial for a family friend. Kennethson did not work on this scale again, turning instead to work specifically designed to be seen in a 'domestic' environment. This was, in part, a practical decision, as he had been forced to leave work behind when the family moved to Oundle, Northamptonshire, in 1954, as it had been too difficult to move. In the main, however, Kennethson

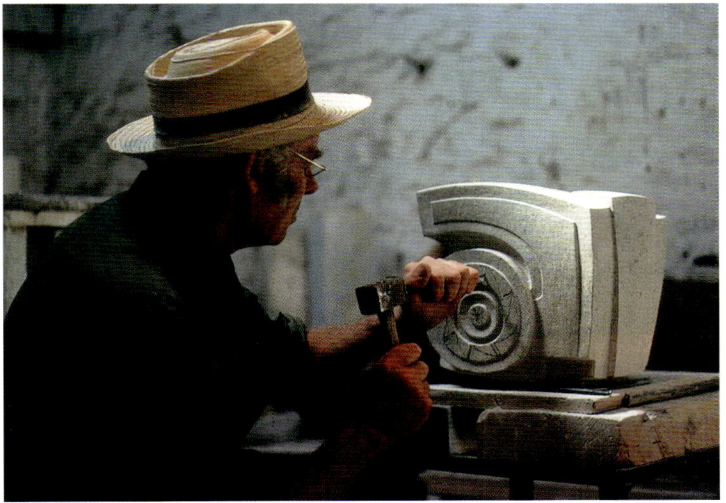

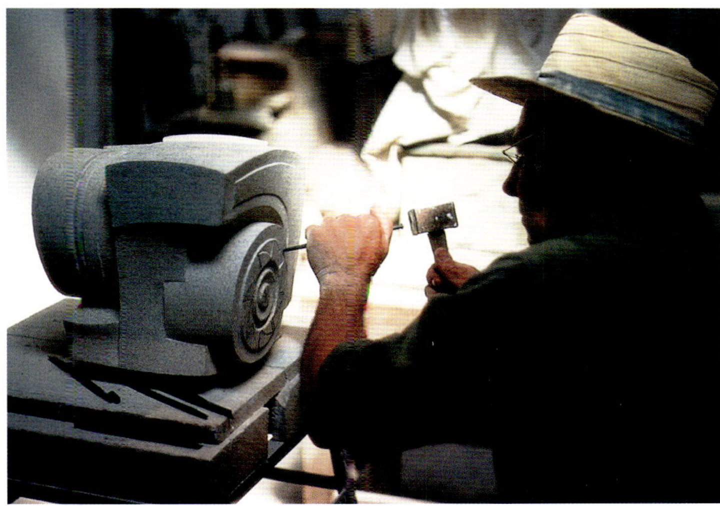

Fig. 9
The sculptor at work, September 1976

did not like to see his sculptures weather and take on an unintended pattern and colour that would dull the sharp, shallow incisions that are such an important element of his work.

In 1946 a visitor to Uffington, Godfrey Pilkington (who later founded the Piccadilly Gallery in London), organized an exhibition of some of Kennethson's works in Bristol, which led to his participation the following year in an Arts Council touring exhibition entitled *Sculpture in the Home*. However, as he was to do throughout his life, Kennethson did not use this exposure to try to find representation at a major gallery. The work was everything and the less that got in the way of him making it the better. Instead he followed the advice of his friend and neighbour in Uffington, John Betjeman, who had drawn his attention to a job as an art master at Oundle School, for which he thought George – with his enthusiasm for talking about art, especially with young people – would be well suited and that would also provide the means to enable him to carry on sculpting.

At first George, Eileen and their five sons lived in a small house in the middle of the town, with a converted chicken shed near by acting as a studio. A *Couple* (plate 32), dating from this period, shows Kennethson's stylistic progress: while the rounded forms are still somewhat indebted to Moore and Hepworth's works of the 1920s, the hands (something of a speciality), the faces and the flat cap turned into a sleek sculptural element are all distinctly his own. He made a number of these works throughout his career (plates 12, 14 and 18), but this piece is especially poignant, as it seems to represent George and Eileen, both bodies turned straight on, looking ahead together to the future.

In 1959 the Kennethsons found a disused brewery on the edge of Oundle that at last provided enough space for the family as well as sculpture workshops for George and a painting studio for Eileen. Their lives began to fall into a routine that would shape the decades to come. George's 'real' day began in the early evening, after teaching, when he would go to his studio, with only cassettes of piano concertos and the sound of a hammer and chisel for company.

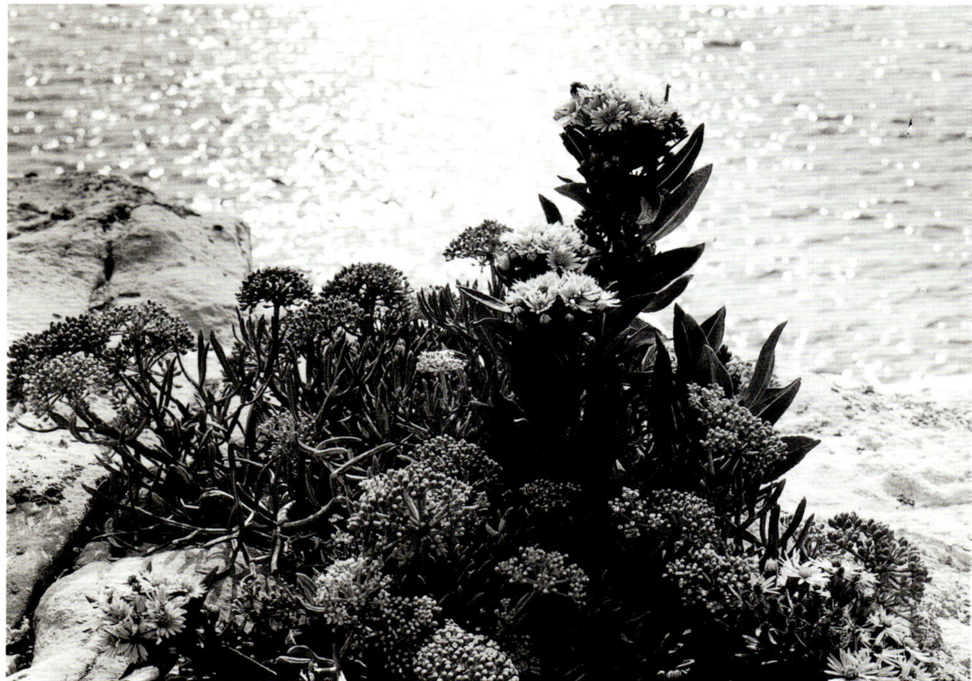

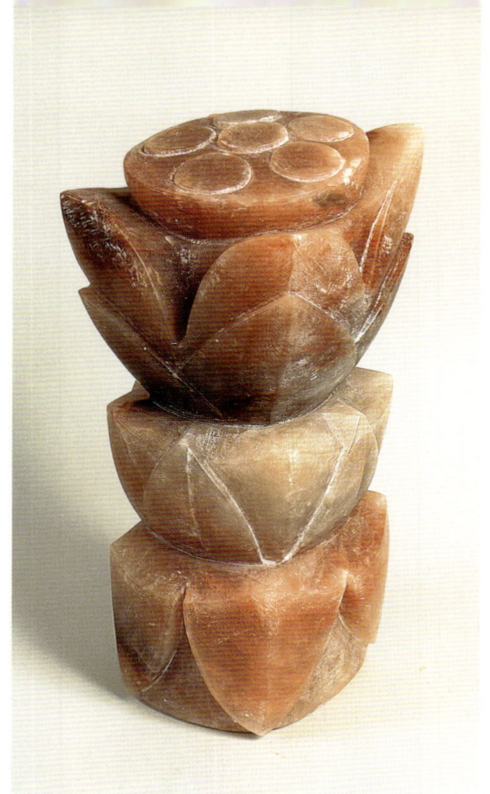

Fig. 10
Rock plants, with sea behind, *c.* 1970
Photograph taken by the artist

Fig. 11
Tall Flower and Leaf
c. 1970
Alabaster
43 x 18 x 20 cm (17 x 7 x 8 in.)
Estate of the artist

Kennethson's *œuvre* can be loosely divided between two main themes: landscape and the human body. Representations of the entire landscape, such as *Landscape with Sun* (plate 26), are quite rare, as he felt painting was more suited to trying to capture the overall sense of space and air. Instead, he splits nature into single elements: waves (representing the sea), flowers and plants (land) and birds (air).

Kennethson's flower forms (plate 19) have an almost imaginary quality to them, as if they were lush, narcotic lotuses from a nineteenth-century Romantic poem. Yet they are based very much on the simple, ancient plant forms that flourish in the wind and salt-laden rain of the English coast (figs. 10 and 11). For these pieces Kennethson worked almost exclusively in Staffordshire alabaster, as it could be polished smooth until light became trapped like moisture and the stone seemed to glisten with ripeness.

Throughout history birds have always stood as metonyms for the flux and endless movement of the natural world, and Kennethson often combined bird forms with waves to the point that it became indistinguishable where one ended and the other began. Birds also had a symbolic value, often appearing cradled in the arms or sitting on the shoulders of his figures (plate 28). As Kennethson himself wrote, "I suppose surely almost everyone is fascinated by birds and the flight of birds. It's partly empathy, which plays a big part in the arts, and with birds in flight it is really to do with freedom. You have sympathy with something moving in a different medium, the air; the feeling of life in another dimension."

Kennethson's wave pieces are perhaps some of his most significant works and in many ways bear comparison with Hepworth's sculpture in the years following her move to St Ives, Cornwall.

Since childhood, Kennethson had spent nearly every summer by the sea. From the late 1930s onwards he and Eileen stayed on the Isle of Purbeck, Dorset, where the interaction of the sea on the coastline provided plenty of inspiration for photographs and drawings (fig. 13). Other attractions were the local quarries, which had been producing material for sculpture, as well as building, for centuries (fig. 12). Here, George could look out over the sea and instantly envisage how he might 'translate' its movement and power into stone. Yet, whereas Hepworth focuses on the fluidity of water, which almost envelops the landscape in an embrace, Kennethson's wave pieces are about the clash of the sea with the coastline. This physical confrontation is realized in sharp, geometric forms, the waves becoming almost mechanical, like cogs and gears, as they turn and tighten in on themselves and grind against the shore. The success of these pieces, in their Modernist evocation of the forces at work along Britain's jagged coastline, should see them stand as counterpoint to Hepworth's more fluid vision, and, as such, they are a significant contribution to British art in the twentieth century.

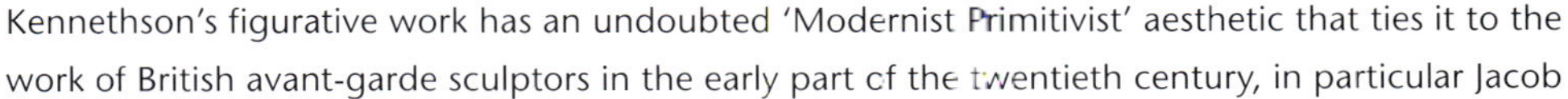

Kennethson's figurative work has an undoubted 'Modernist Primitivist' aesthetic that ties it to the work of British avant-garde sculptors in the early part of the twentieth century, in particular Jacob

Fig. 12
Stone Quarry
c. 1970
Pencil and ink wash on paper, initialled
34 x 24 cm (13½ x 9½ in.)

Fig. 13
Abstracted Figure, Waves and Rocks
Mid 1960s
Pen and ink with wash on paper, initialled
18.5 x 21 cm (7¼ x 8¼ in.)

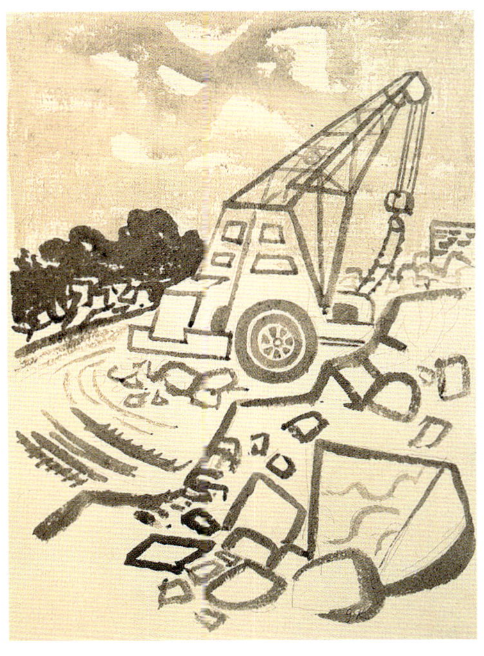

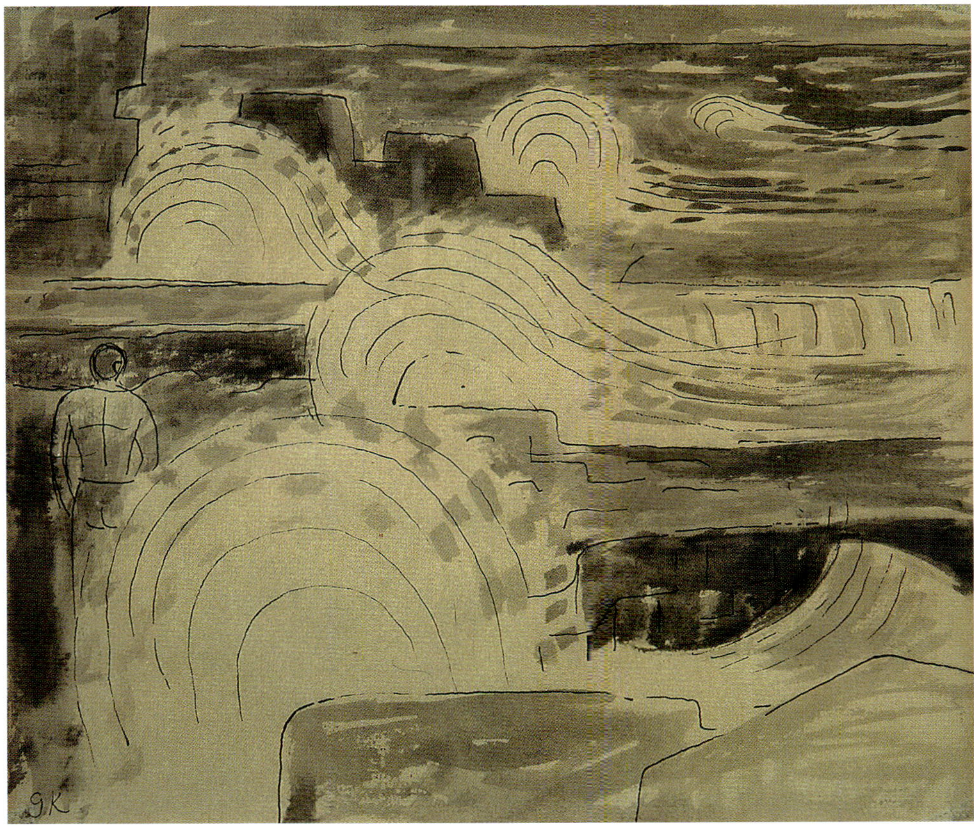

Epstein, Henri Gaudier-Brzeska and Frank Dobson, the early carvings of Moore and Hepworth – indeed, the very artists whose work caused Kennethson to give up painting. However, there is something Byzantine or medieval about them, too, especially in the way in which an almost infinite range of ideas and subjects is expressed within a limited formal vocabulary based on conventional emblematic themes. The idea of a self-imposed limitation of style and form is another aspect of Kennethson's work that seems more process-driven and therefore contemporary in concept.

Although Kennethson was influenced by medieval architectural sculpture, particularly the exteriors of the abbey church at Vézelay and Autun Cathedral, he made only one overtly religious sculpture throughout his career, a *Crucifixion*, now in the church of St Joseph in Emsdetten, Germany. His inspiration for his silent, almost hieratic figures seems to come more from Romantic literature, with their Orientalist clothes and hairstyles and inscrutable expressions. It is as if they are effigies from lost imaginary kingdoms, such as that of Shelley's *Ozymandias*.

Set against these timeless, non-European figures are the pieces that are evidently based on direct observation: of men at work and people at the market, or on buses or the Tube; street entertainers and circus performers; girls seen through hairdressers' windows, their elaborate hairstyles having the same cascading movement of planes and volumes as waves reaching the shore. While drawing from life, Kennethson was already separating out the 'everyday' into something more universal, but, interestingly, he would often retain certain details – such as the flat caps worn by the men in his *Couples* or by his *Travellers* – that seem to hold them in a specific time and place. As such, Kennethson's figures constantly defy definition, being seemingly 'Modernist Primitive', medieval, Oriental and very English all at the same time. Kennethson's figures are almost always expressionless, their faces like masks, their eyes empty and without pupils. This, too, allows the works to remain fugitive, denying only a single reading. They represent a floating world, tied down only by their physical presence. As the sculptor himself commented, "It might be fair to say that [my figurative works] are translations from what was seen, not imagined, but perhaps that's not an accurate thing to say because what you see you imagine. You pick out imaginary themes."

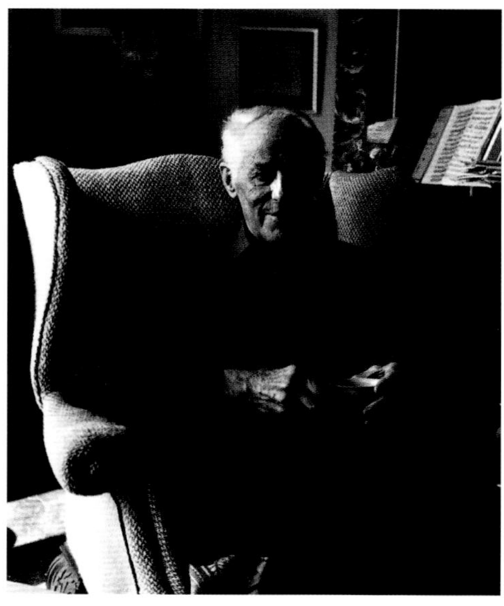

Fig. 14
Portrait of Jim Ede in George Kennethson's drawing-room in Oundle, *c.* 1967

Although Kennethson's subject-matter and, to an extent, his style (sometimes angular and geometric, other times fluid and smooth) change, one aspect of his work remains constant: the presence of the original block of stone. He always attempted to remove as little as possible from each block in order to retain the sense of its original form. Rather than ordering blocks of stone of a particular size for a particular image he had in mind, Kennethson looked for blocks in the dimensions and proportions he thought would be most useful. What he then made from each one depended to an extent on the character of the stone itself and the rhythms he found within it.

The harder limestones, such as Clipsham or Hornton, often yielded forms defined by angular planes and deep cuts, with detail carved in low relief, whereas softer materials, such as alabaster, give way to smoother, more flowing shapes, articulated with delicate incisions that appear to have been drawn with a pen. Kennethson also used the various colours he found running through the stone to draw attention to certain elements of the piece. Angles and curves in works such as *Girl*

Resting and *Reclining Figure* (plates 7 and 29) are further articulated by the brown streaks running through the normally grey Clipsham stone. Alabaster pieces such as *Crayfish*, *Rock and Wave Form* or *Boy with a Bird* (plates 13, 28 and 31), are shot through with brown, pink and white, each of which responds differently in light. Indeed, light is a key element to these works. They are carved in such a way that details, planes and volumes often only truly come alive when light permeates the stone, illuminating it from within.

Kennethson mostly used local stones – Hornton from Banbury, Oxfordshire, Clipsham from Stamford, Lincolnshire, alabaster from Staffordshire and marble and limestone from his beloved Isle of Purbeck – and in the course of over fifty years of carving he got to know their specific qualities intimately. 'Truth to materials' in sculpture could be achieved only through working with them, day after day over a long period of time.

Despite Kennethson's relative isolation in Oundle, his work was shown throughout his career, often in small solo exhibitions in provincial museums and galleries. The most important of these was a retrospective, *Translations from Life and Nature: Stone Carvings 1950–1985*, at Peterborough Museum and Art Gallery in 1986, the catalogue of which contained a number of statements from the normally reticent sculptor. However, the wider recognition in his lifetime was largely due to the pioneering collector and connoisseur Jim Ede (fig. 14), whom he met at Kettle's Yard in Cambridge, Ede's house that by then was open to the public. The two men struck up an instant friendship, based on their impassioned belief that there lies within anything – a pebble found on a beach or a sculpture by Brancusi – a simplicity of form or an economy of line that in themselves can inspire a sense of harmony often missing from the modern world. George and Eileen would often drive to Kettle's Yard to fetch Jim and his wife, Helen, give them lunch in Oundle and then drive them back to Cambridge in time for them to open the house to visitors at 2 o'clock.

Fig. 15
The Dancer Room at Kettle's Yard, Cambridge, showing (from left to right) Christopher Wood's *Landscape with Figures*, Henri Gaudier-Brzeska's *Dancer* and George Kennethson's *Construction – Birds*

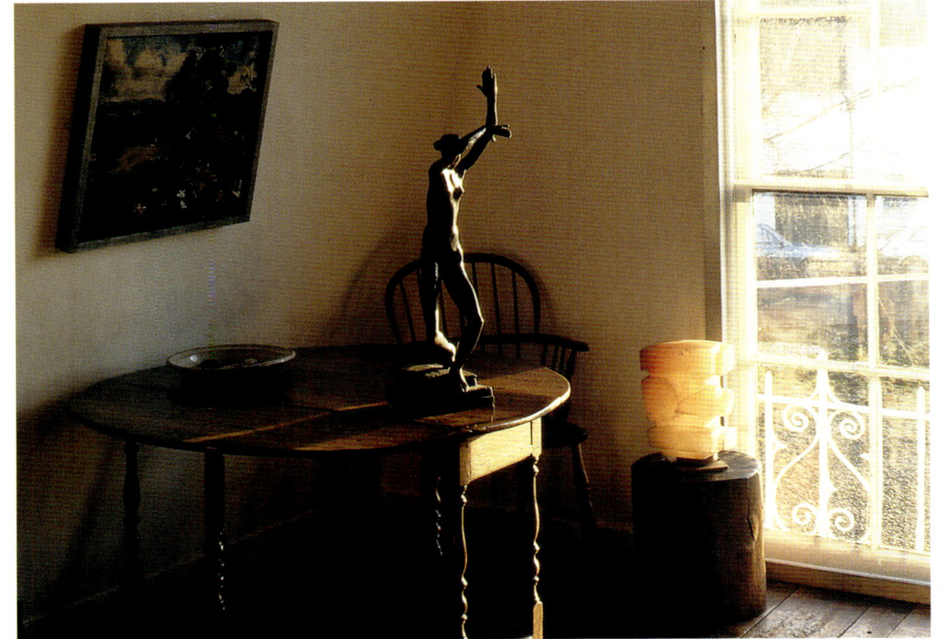

Ede, a former curator at the Tate Gallery, London, and Assistant Secretary of the Contemporary Art Society, was an extremely influential figure in Modernism in Britain in the 1930s, almost single-handedly reviving interest in the work of Henri Gaudier-Brzeska, as well as supporting such artists as Ben Nicholson and Barbara Hepworth in their early careers. Ede bought two of Kennethson's more abstract alabaster pieces for Kettle's Yard, where he planned to display them alongside works by Brancusi and Gaudier-Brzeska (fig. 15). *Construction – Birds* is still on display in the museum, set in a typically 'casual' way on a low cylindrical plinth by a window so that the afternoon light suffuses the stone, highlighting the intersection of volumes and planes (figs. 15 and 17). Kennethson also gave Ede two more pieces, which he took to the flat in Edinburgh where he lived out his final years surrounded by his treasures, having finally handed over Kettle's Yard to the University of Cambridge in 1973. One of these works, *Sea Study* of *c.* 1974, was donated by Ede to the Scottish National Gallery of Modern Art, with the other remaining in the family.

Ede had 'discovered' the work of Henri Gaudier-Brzeska in the 1920s, at a time when the artist remained virtually unknown outside a small, London-based group of artists, writers and collectors, despite a career that had burnt very brightly before his death aged only twenty-three. The Tate had been offered Gaudier-Brzeska's estate, but had bought only a couple of works. Ede acquired as many of the remaining pieces as he could and then set about restoring the reputation of this young sculptor who had been so influential on such artists as Dobson, Moore, Skeaping and Hepworth. In 1931 Ede published a biography of Gaudier-Brzeska, *Savage Messiah*, the first edition of which Kennethson owned and read often.

Ede undoubtedly saw a number of similarities between Kennethson and Gaudier-Brzeska, not least the single-mindedness that defines both artists' work. Each had started as a painter but, under the influence of non-European 'primitive' art, had turned to sculpture – specifically to carving in stone – in their search for truth and authenticity. Gaudier-Brzeska, in his short career as a sculptor, made only 120 works, whereas Kennethson carved over 400 pieces during the course of over fifty years, and yet there is a remarkable clarity of vision and consistency of purpose in both their *œuvres*.

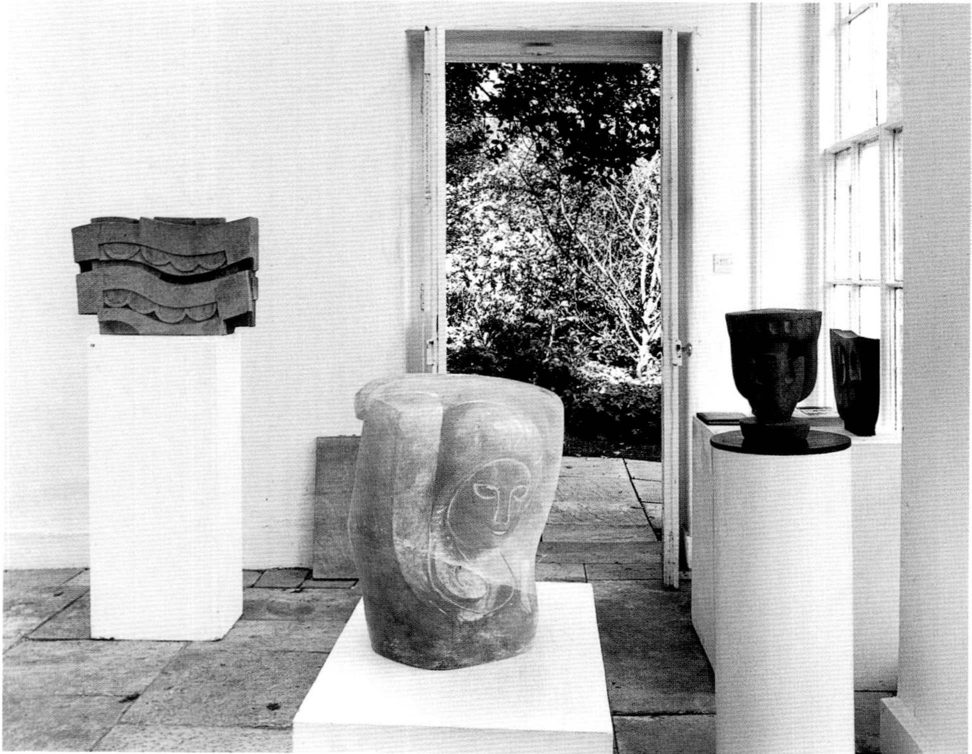

Fig. 16
George Kennethson's solo exhibition at The New Art Centre at Roche Court, Wiltshire, 1993

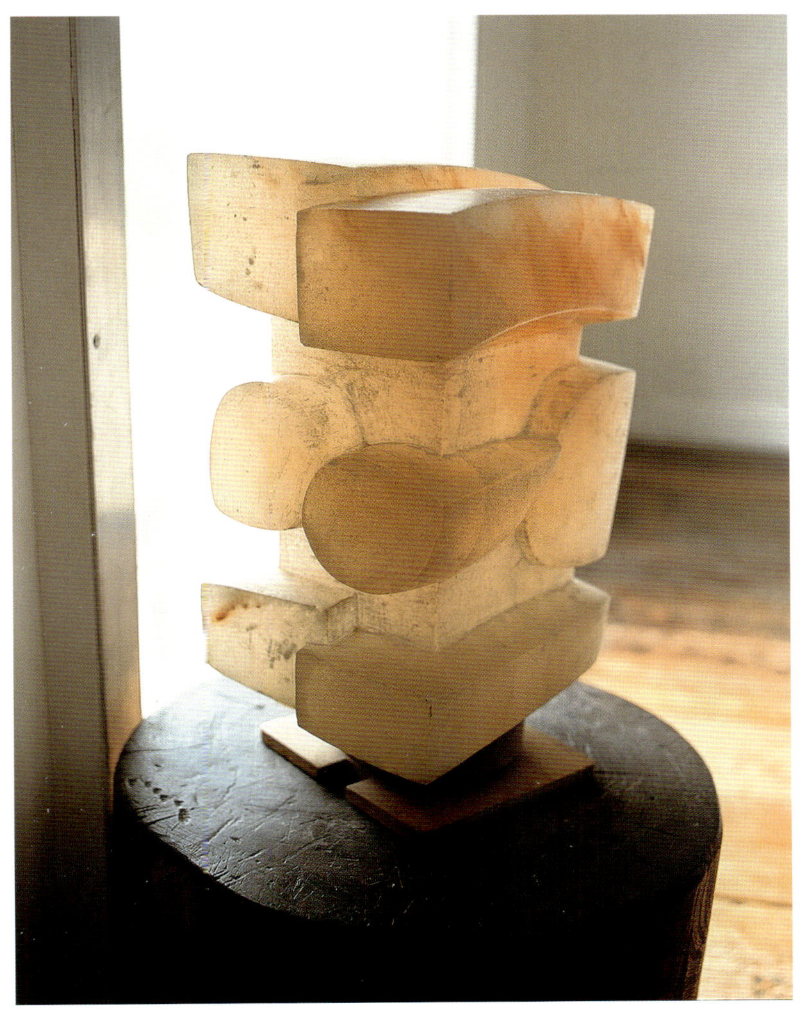

Fig. 17
Construction – Birds, *c.* 1970, in situ at Kettle's Yard, Cambridge

In 1985 Jim Ede introduced Kennethson to Rosanna Wilson Stephens, who was then working at The New Art Centre in Sloane Street, London. This led to a successful solo exhibition at The New Art Centre in 1988. Madeleine Ponsonby, Director of The New Art Centre, was at the time London's leading dealer in Modern British sculpture, specializing in the work of Moore and Hepworth. Suddenly, aged seventy-eight, Kennethson found himself being shown among his better-known contemporaries after years of working in isolation. He continued to exhibit at The New Art Centre after its move to the Roche Court Sculpture Garden in Wiltshire, with his final solo exhibition held in 1993 (fig. 16), just a year before he died.

George Kennethson's work is defined by a sense of purpose and singularity of vision that is remarkable for its coherence and consistency over a career lasting more than five decades. During this time British sculpture moved away from figuration towards abstraction and from direct carving towards construction and (perhaps ironically for someone of Kennethson's generation) back to casting in metal. For all the influence of Post-modernism in the last few decades, art history (or at least the version that drives the art market) remains allied to the traditional model of art moving inexorably forwards in a straight line, from one new 'movement' to the next, and Kennethson's work seemed locked into a particular moment in British Modernism that had long since passed.

In many ways, however Kennethson's art and life *did* represent what was both fashionable in the 1960s and 1970s and what is, to an extent, still an important idea in sculpture today. His work is about *process*, the act of making the work being as important as the resulting object. It was about a daily engagement with his material, through which he developed an almost intuitive feel for the interplay of line and plane, mass and volume that he found within the stones themselves. That Kennethson pursued his vision for over fifty years, producing a body of work that is, on one hand, so consistent and yet, on the other, so varied, makes him truly unique. As Constantin Brancusi said, "To see far, that is one thing. To go there, that is another." As we look back at a century of modern sculpture in Britain, this body of work, concerned with the elemental and eternal, as well as the sheer physical process of carving in stone, stands out all the more because it has become so rare.

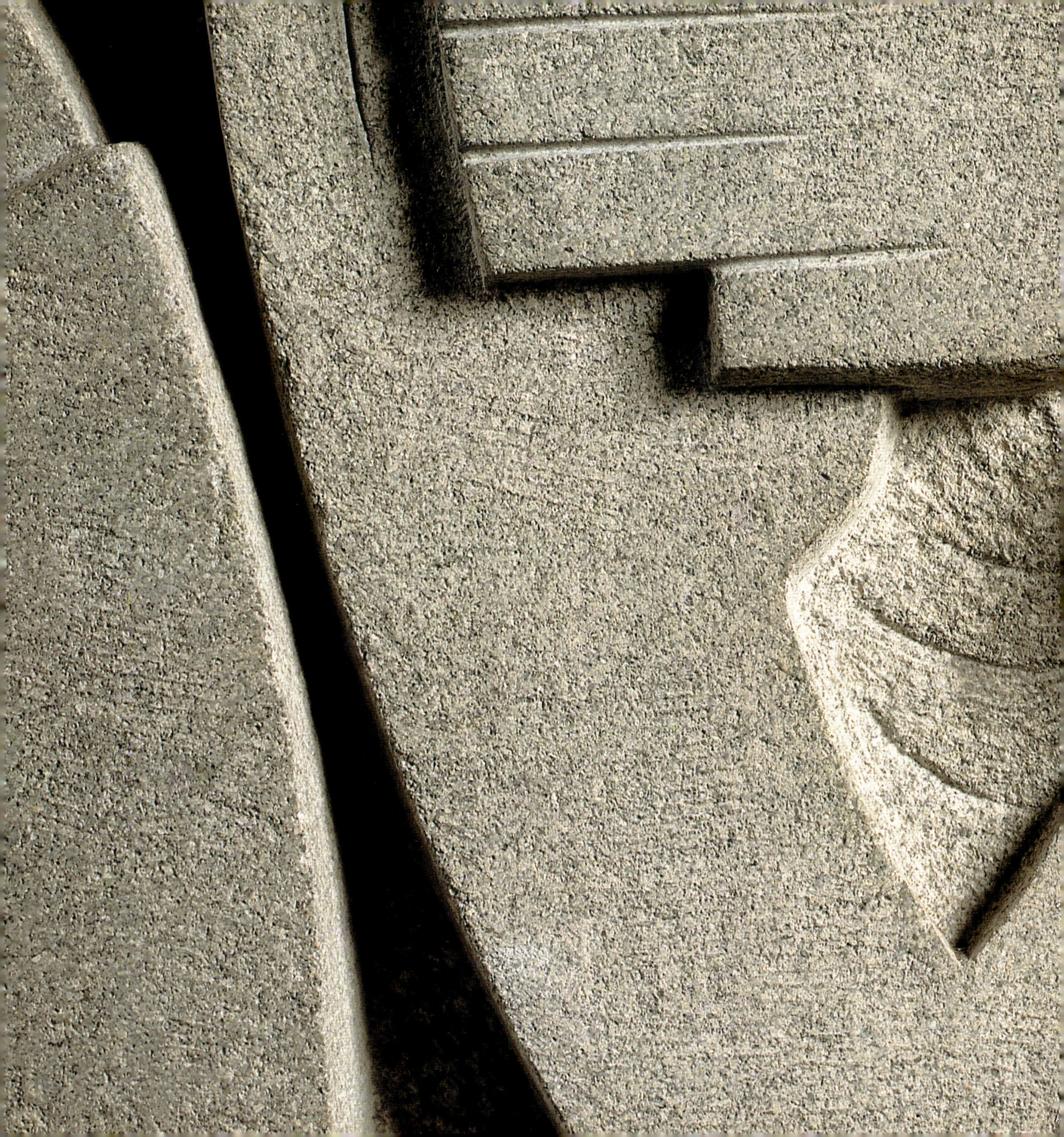

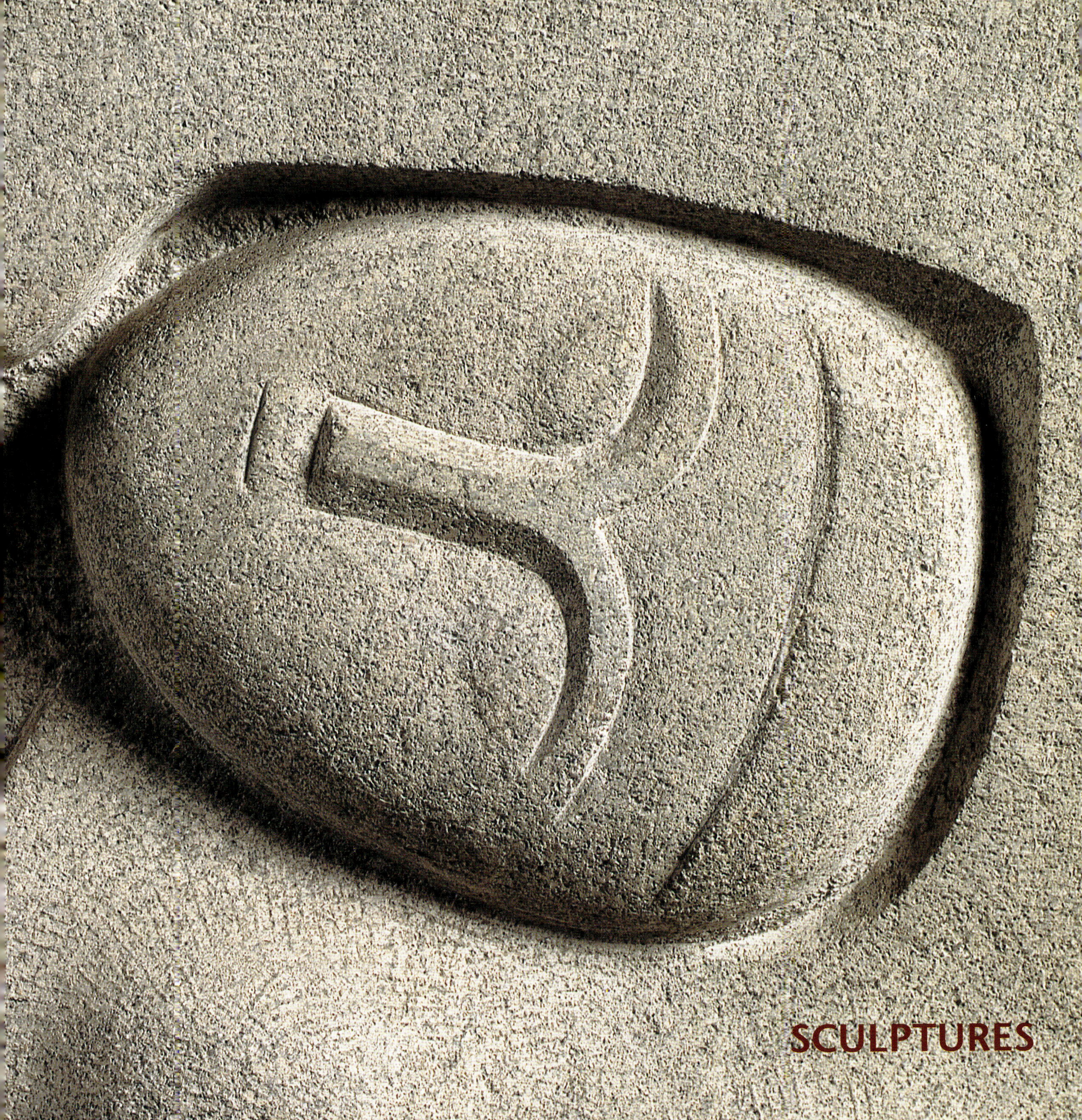

SCULPTURES

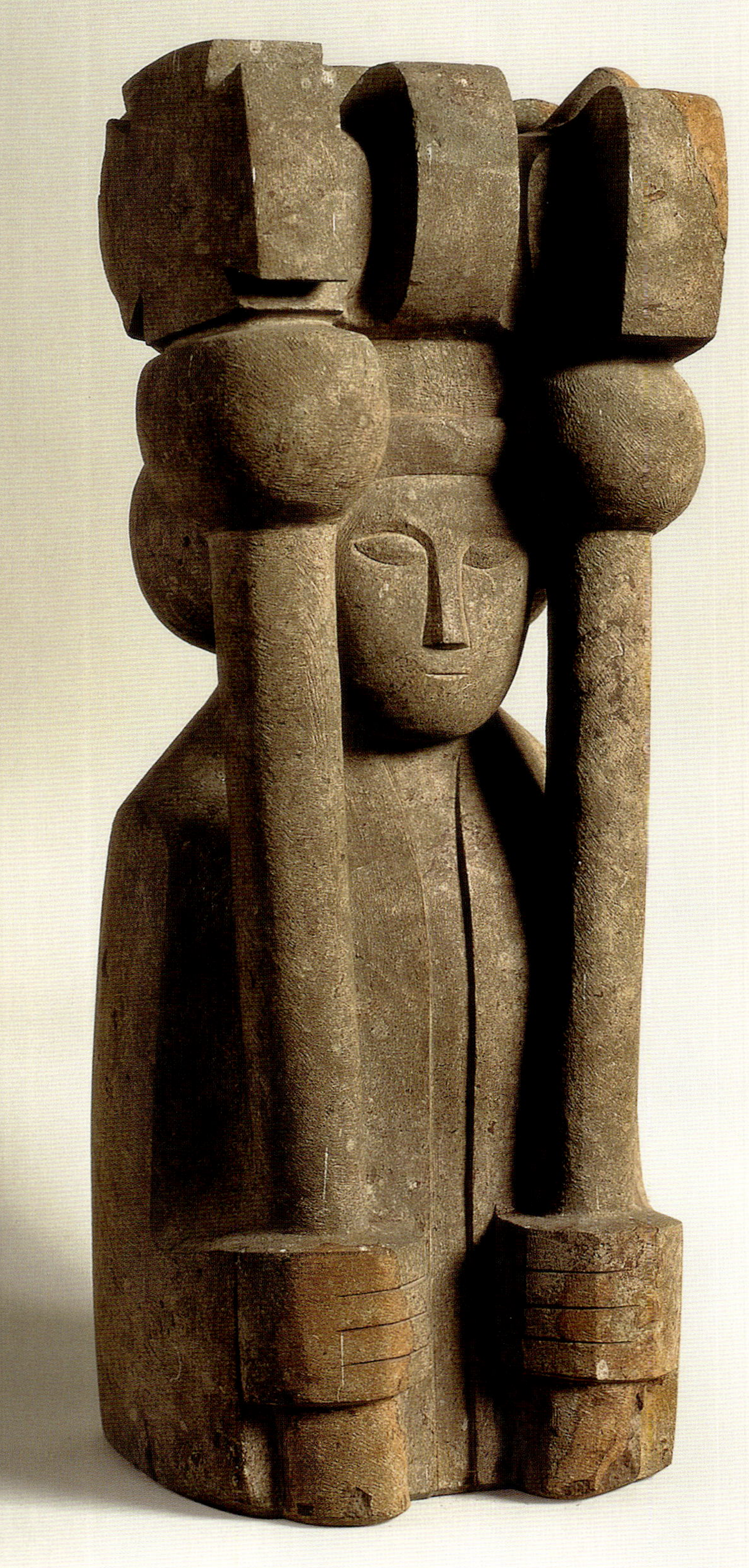

1
Coronation
1952–53
Hornton stone
63.5 x 24 x 23 cm (25 x 9½ x 9 in.)
Estate of the artist: reserve collection

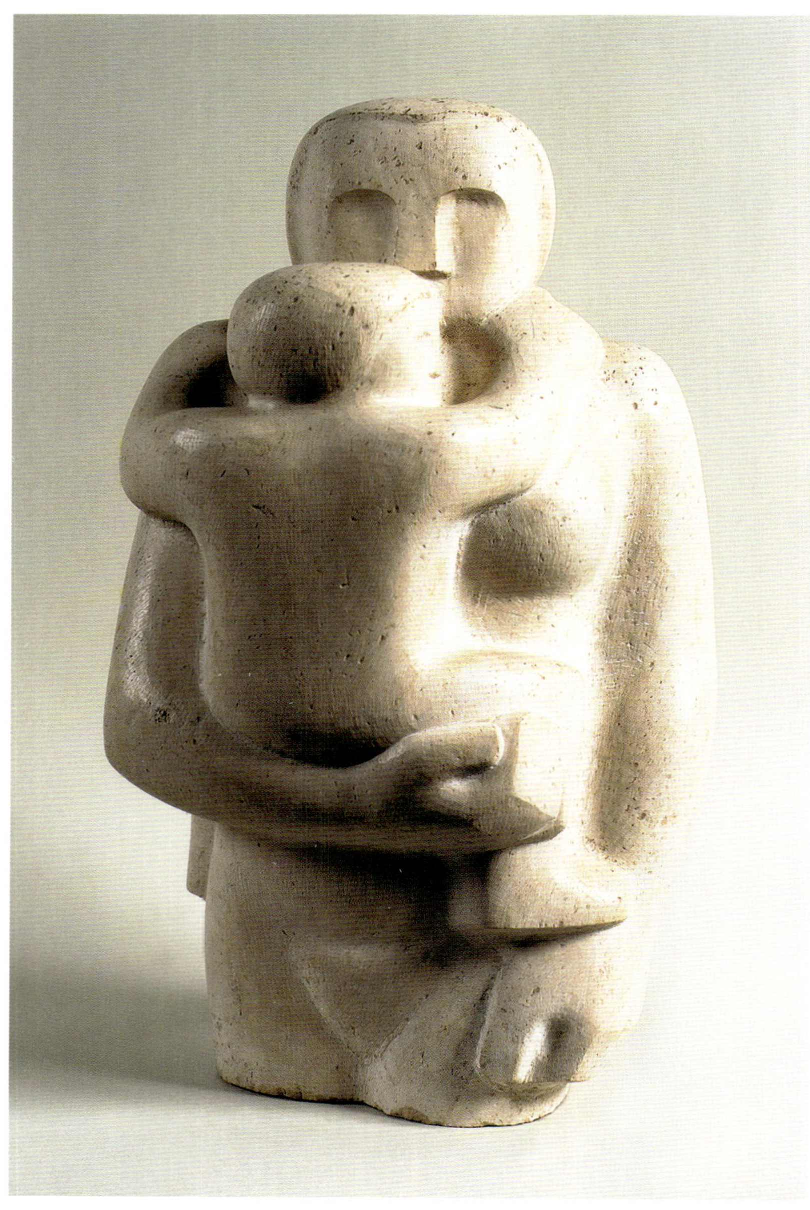

2
Mother and Child
Early 1950s
Hopton Wood stone
58.5 x 33 x 23 cm (23 x 13 x 9 in.)
Estate of the artist: reserve collection

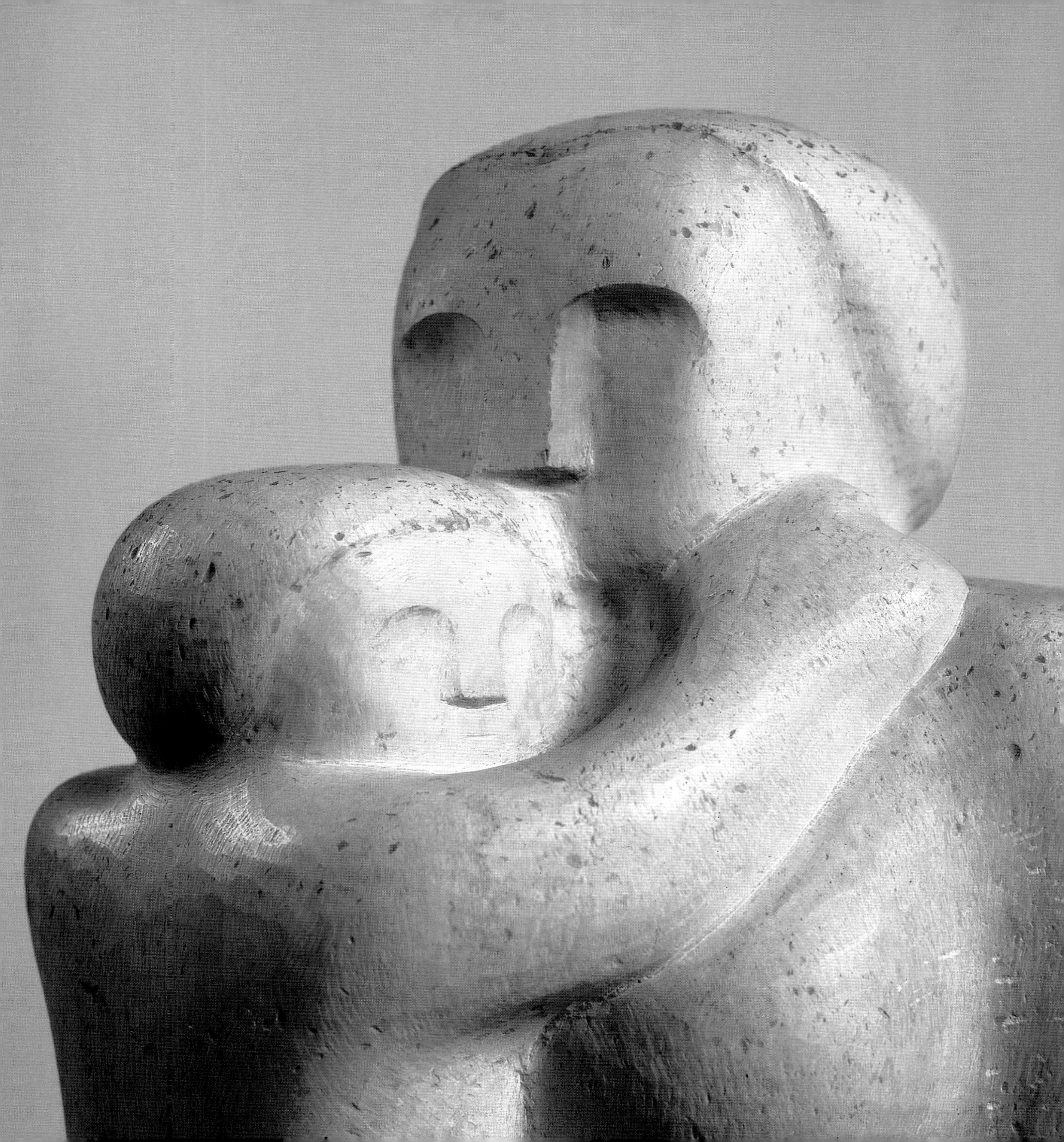

3
Woman with Beads
c. 1975
White Purbeck stone
51 x 28 x 23 cm (20 x 11½ x 9 in.)
Estate of the artist

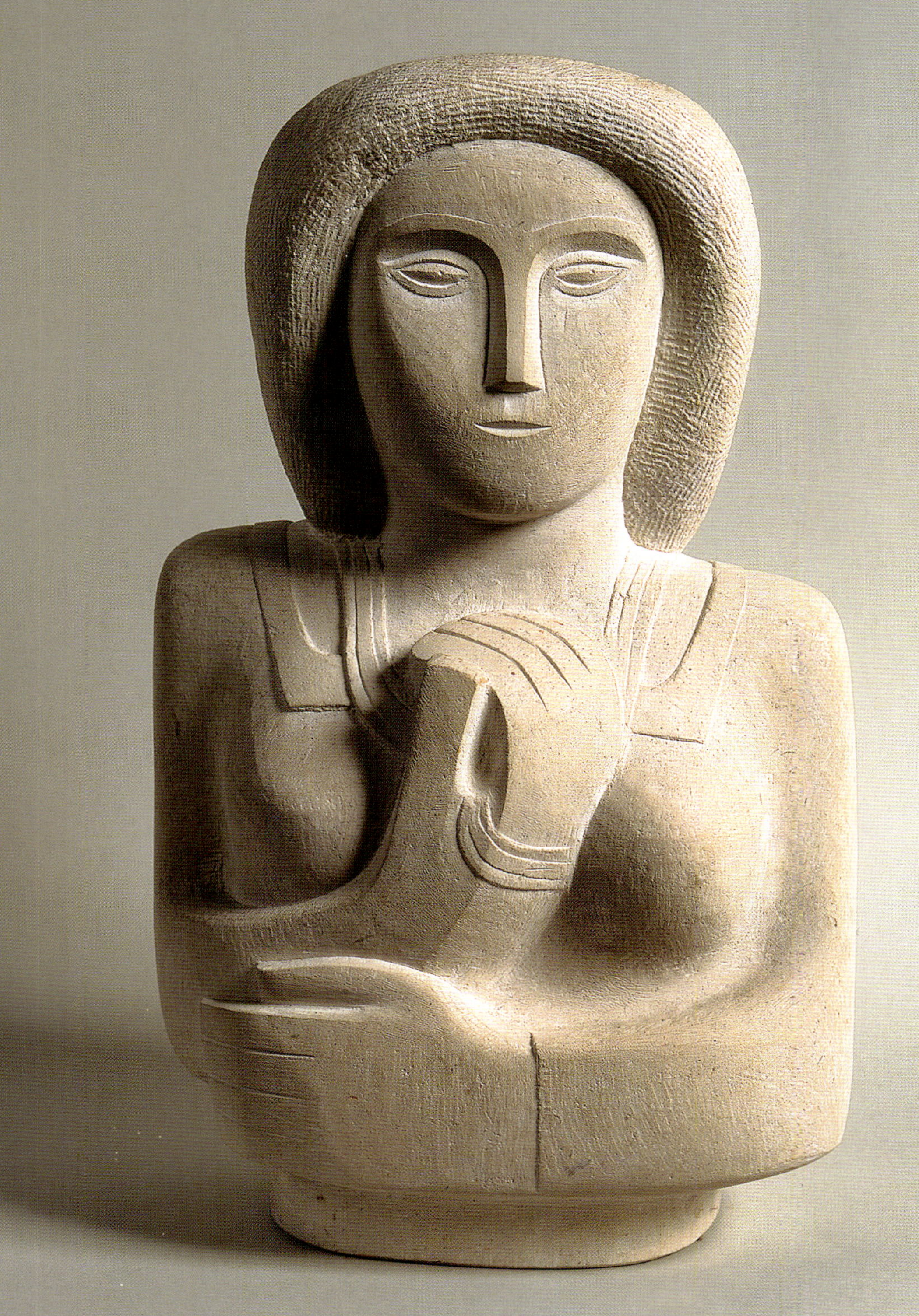

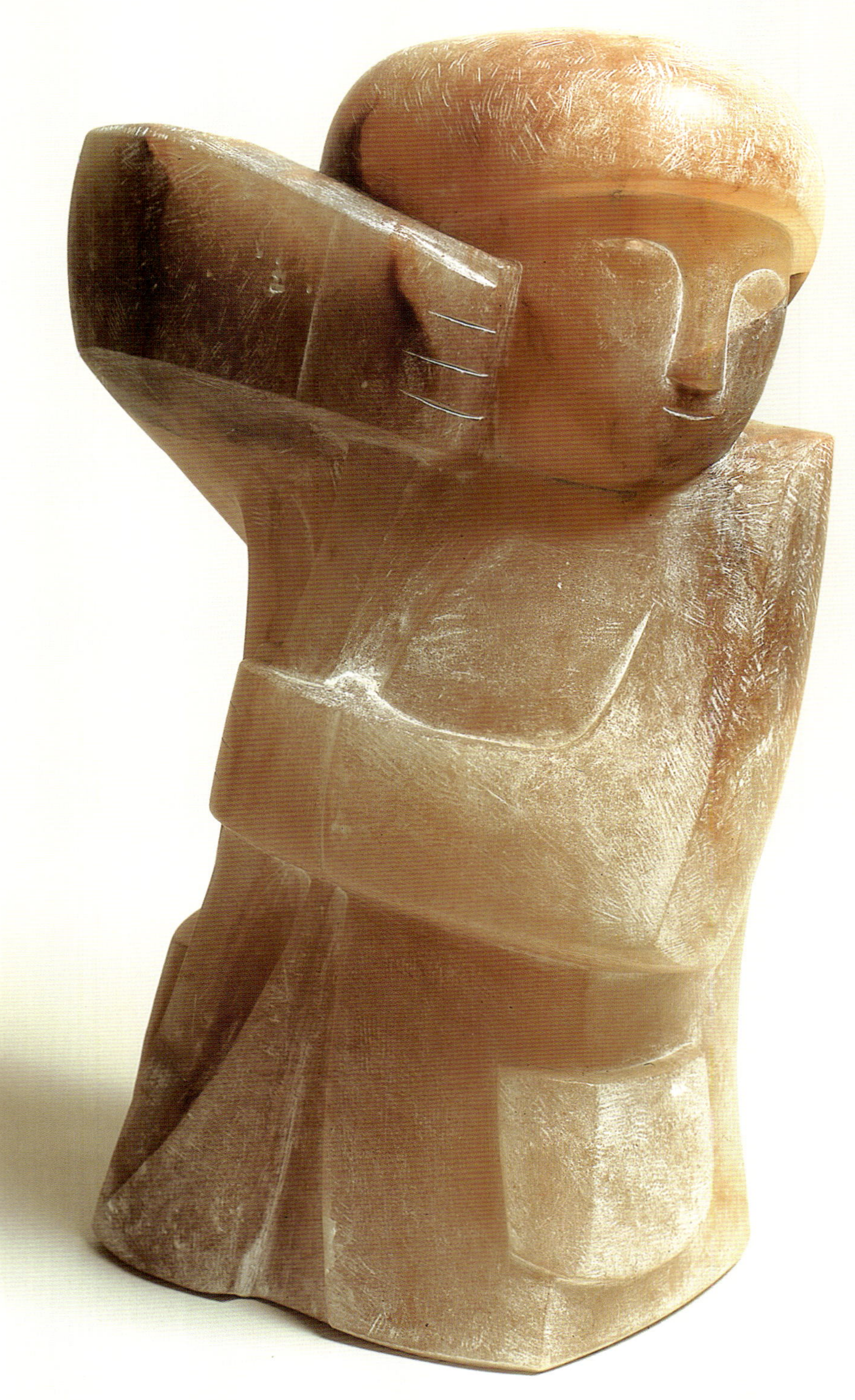

4
Traveller
c. 1980
Alabaster
48 x 25.5 x 19 cm (19 x 10 x 7½ in.)
Cantelo Ellis collection, London

5
Waves
1980s
White alabaster
30.5 x 28 x 23 cm (12 x 11 x 9 in.)
Estate of the artist

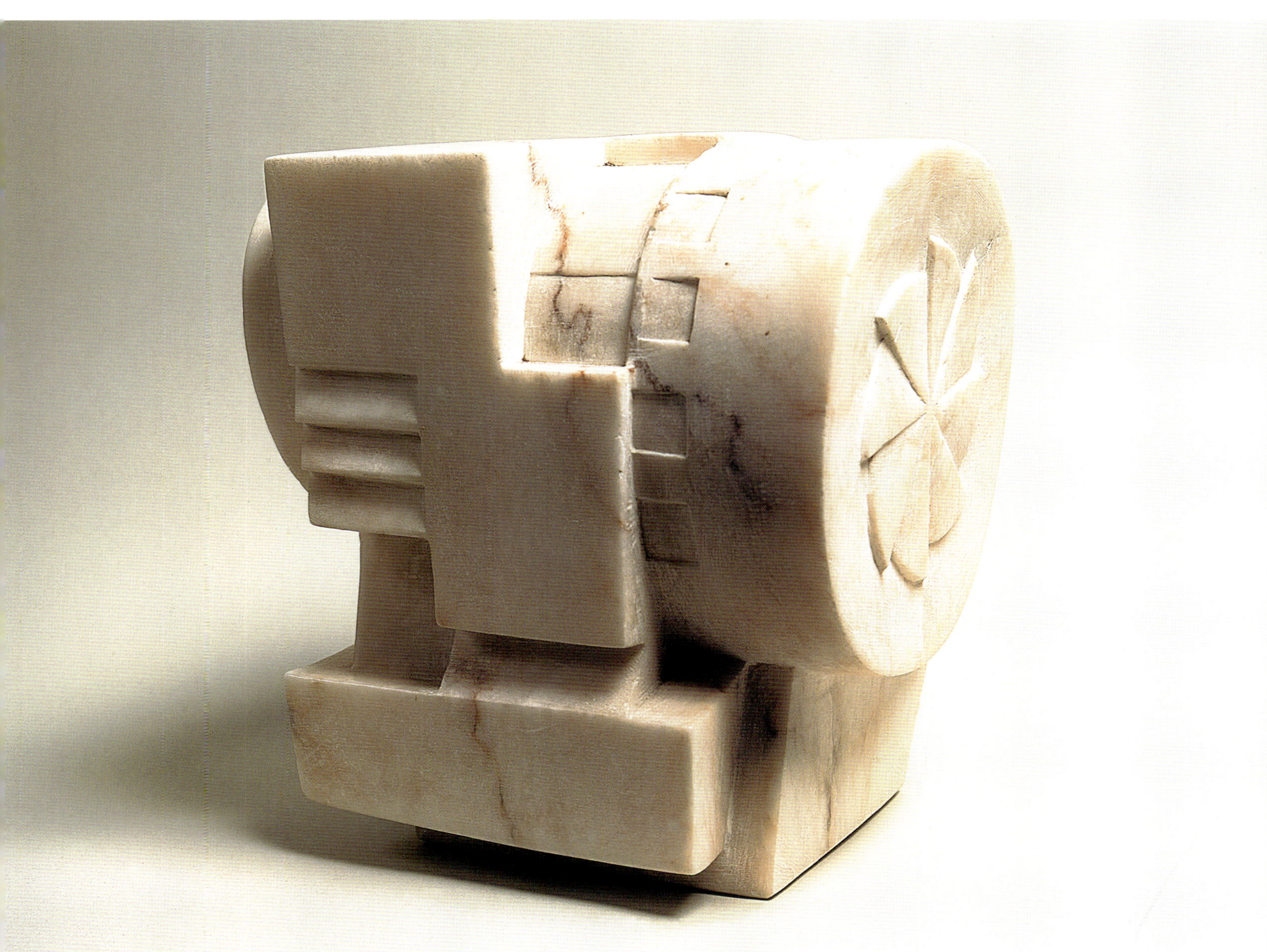

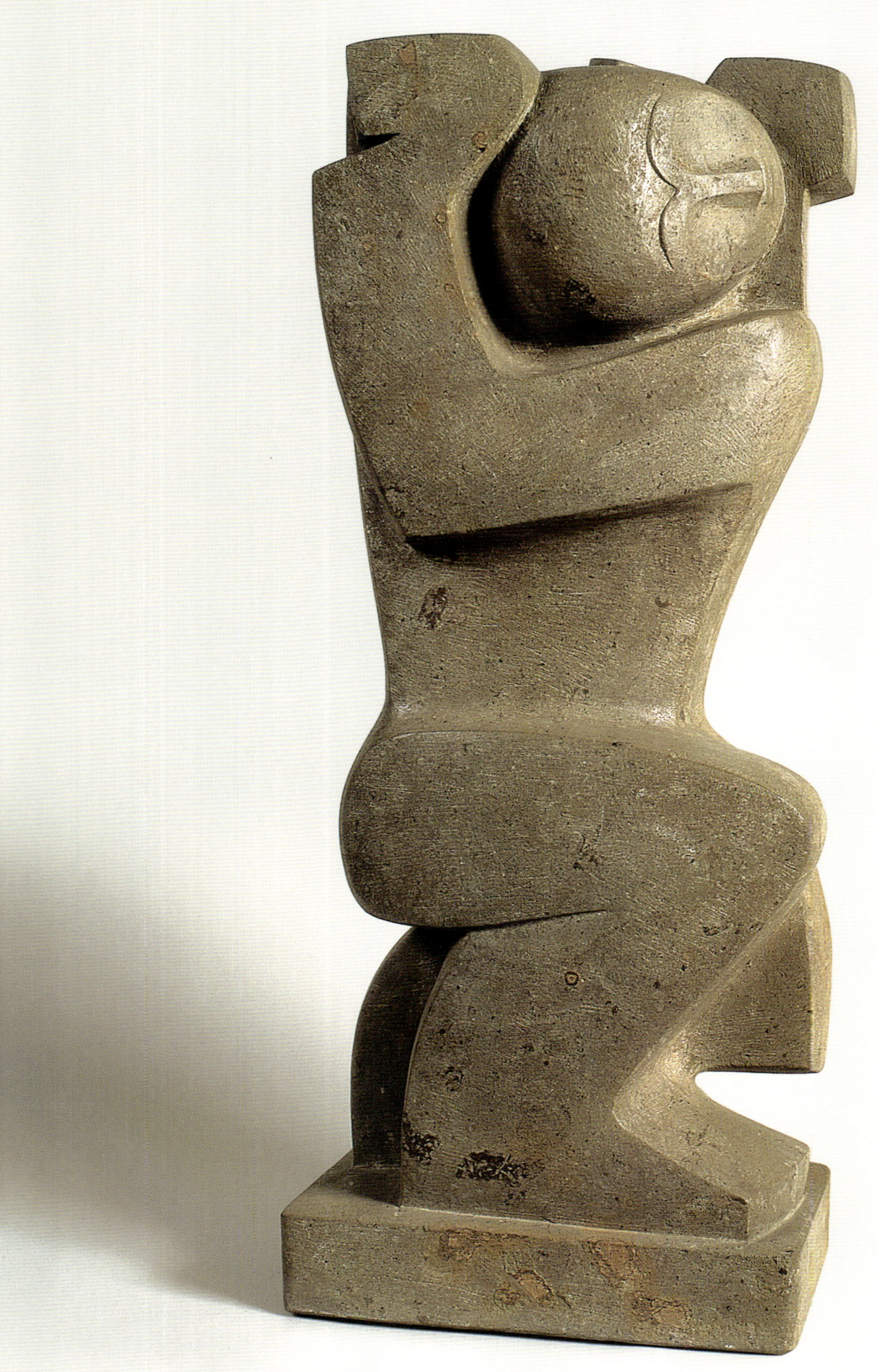

6
Green Man
1970s
Hornton stone
76 x 30.5 x 20 cm (30 x 12 x 8 in.)
Estate of the artist

7
Girl Resting
1970s
Clipsham stone
37 x 46 x 10 cm (14½ x 18 x 4 in.)
Private collection, England

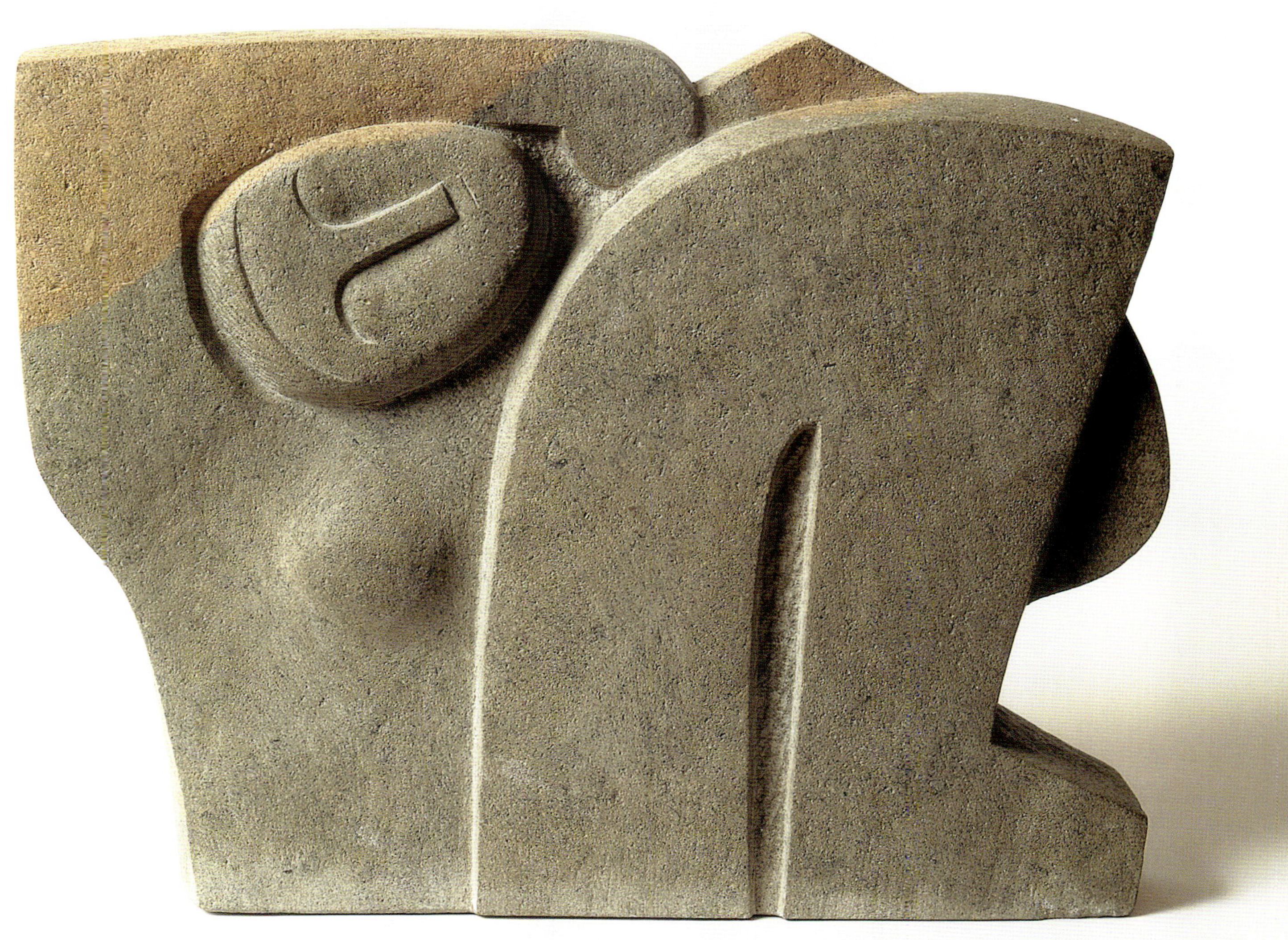

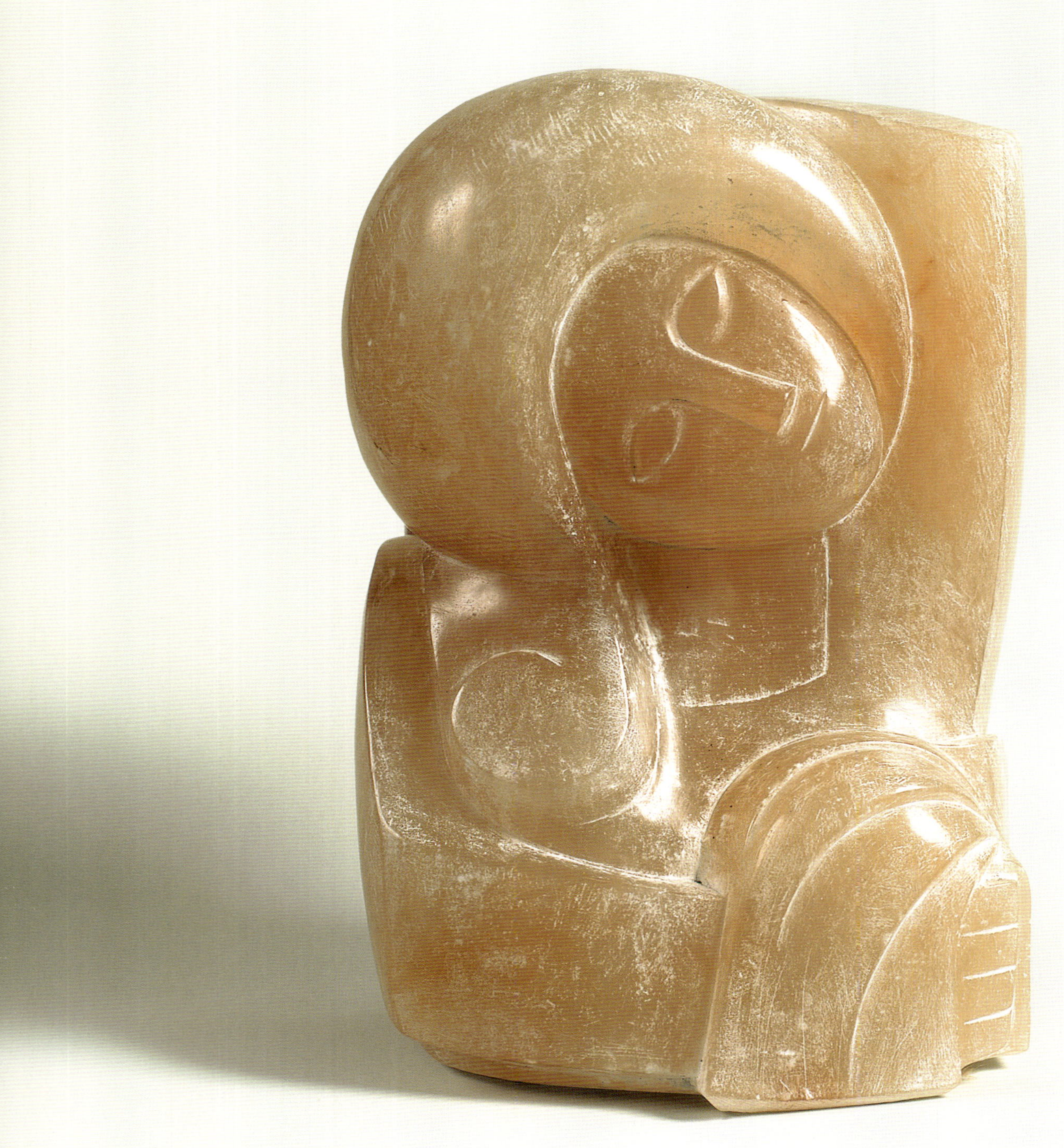

8
Girl with Cloth
Date unknown
Alabaster
40.5 x 26.5 x 25.5 cm (16 x 10½ x 10 in.)
Estate of the artist

9
Seated Figure
c. 1980
Purbeck stone
66 x 26.5 x 26.5 cm (26 x 10½ x 10½ in.)
Estate of the artist

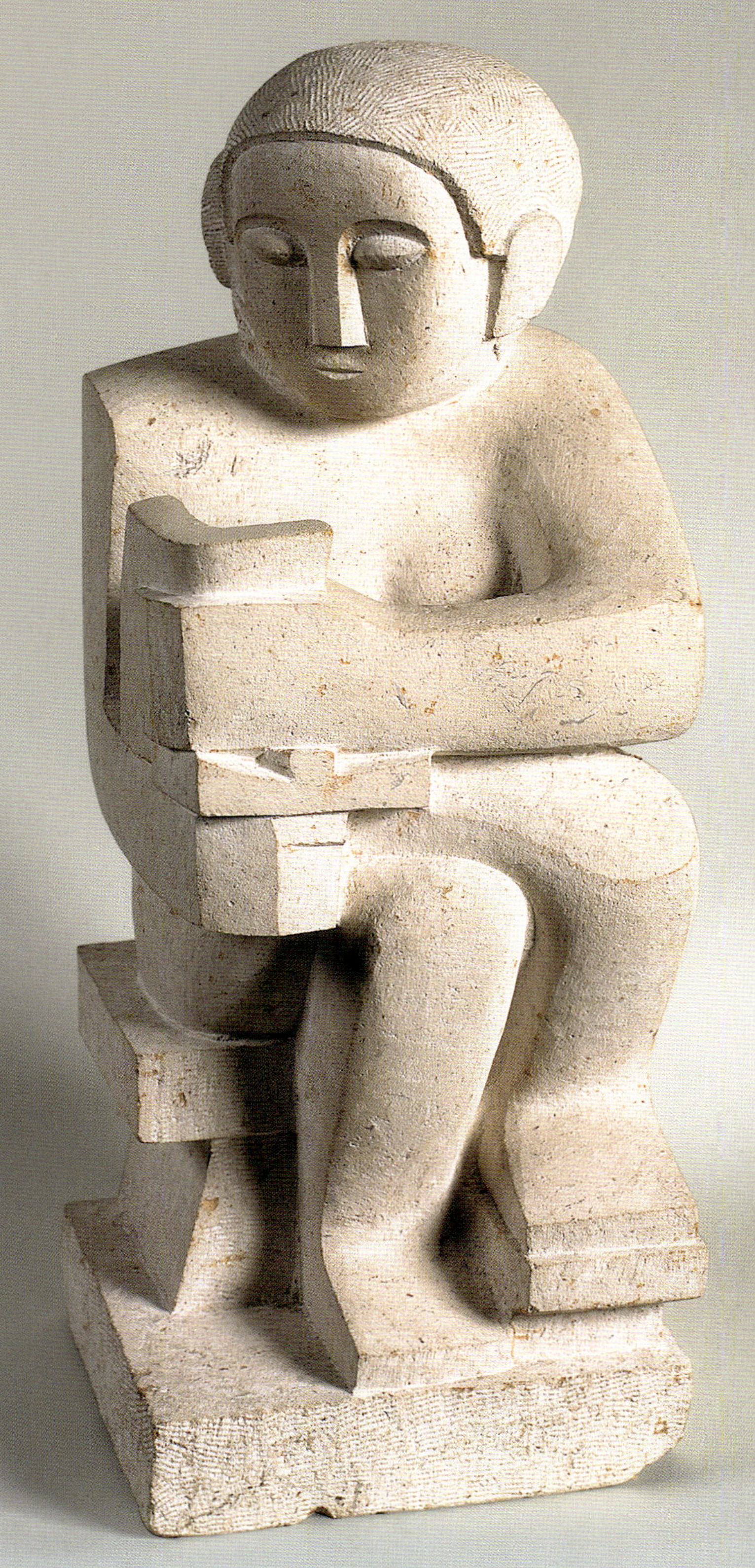

10
Waves
1980s
Clipsham stone
46 x 37 x 15 cm (18 x 14½ x 6 in.)
Estate of the artist: reserve collection

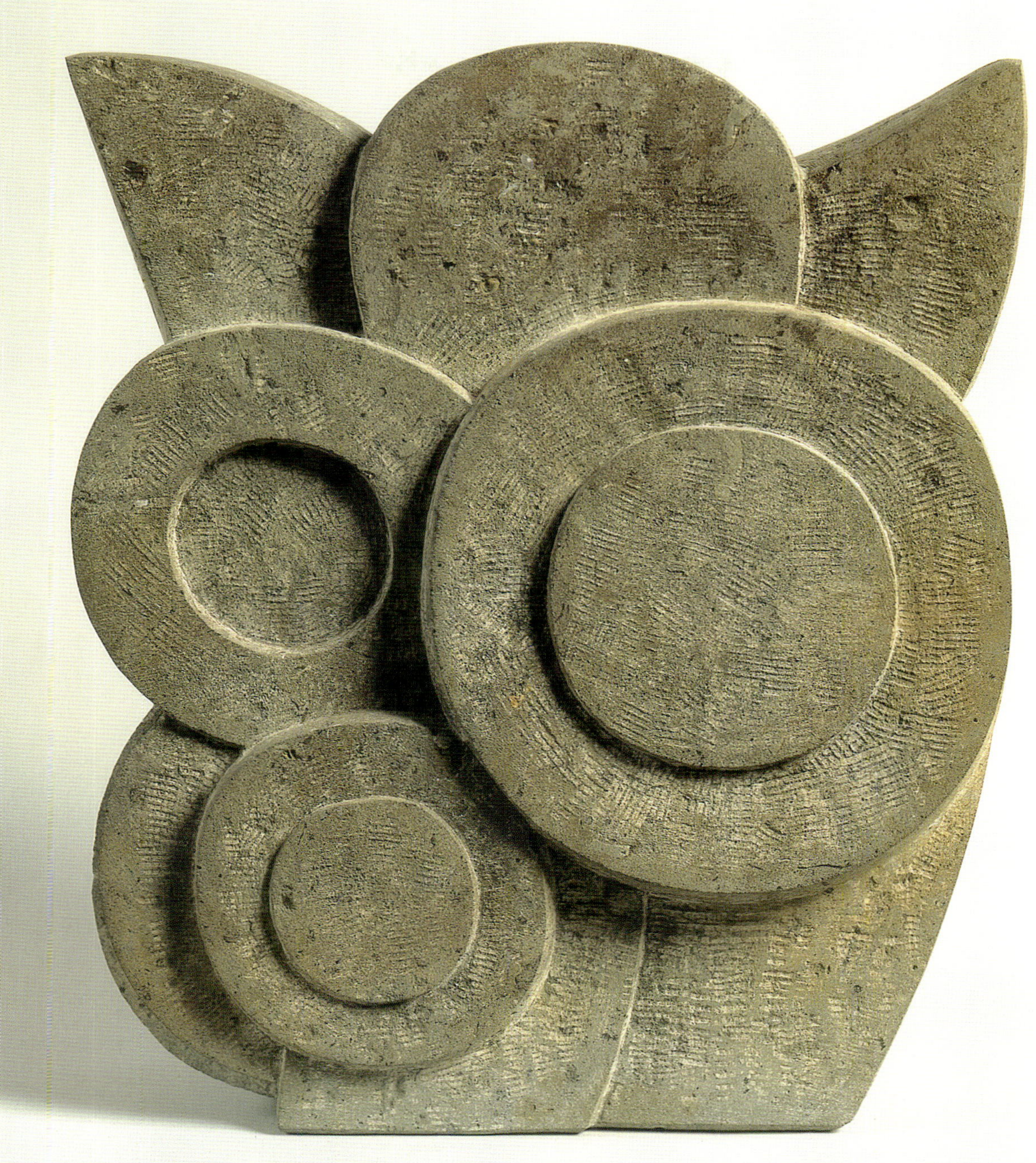

11
Circus Rider
c. 1975–80
Clipsham stone
79 x 29 x 18 cm (31 x 11½ x 7 in.)
Estate of the artist

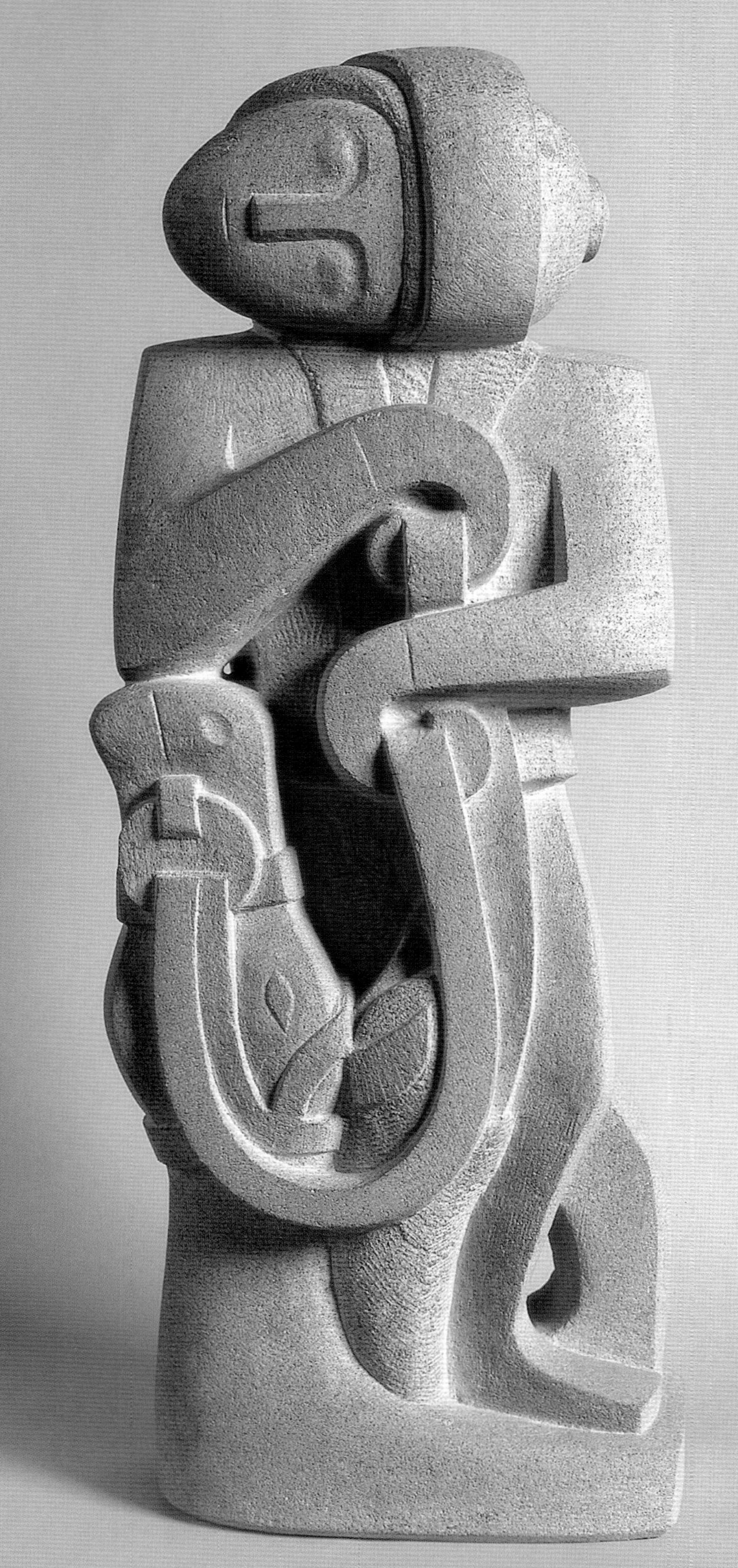

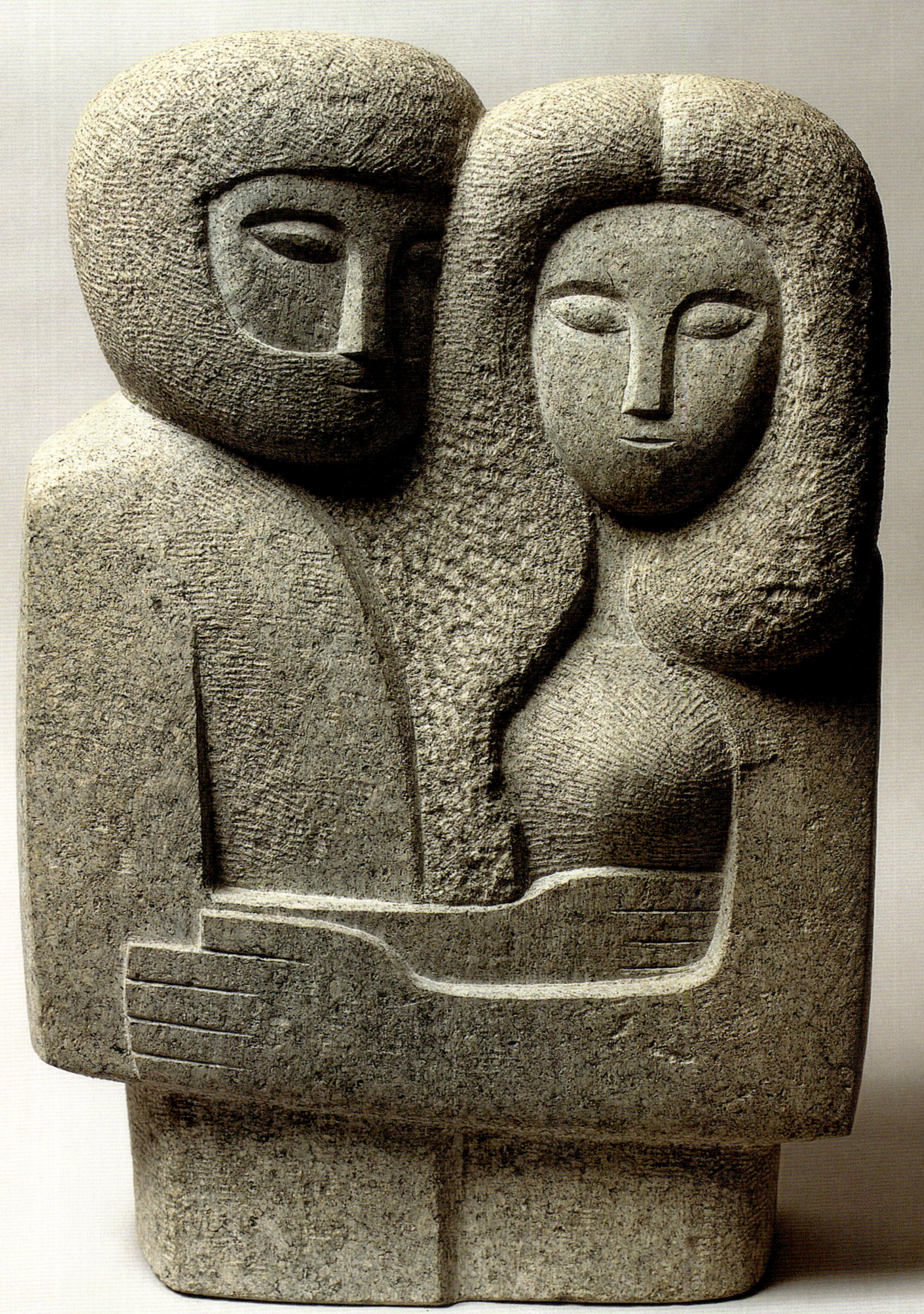

12
Couple
1980s
Clipsham stone
51 x 33 x 14 cm (20 x 13 x 5½ in.)
Estate of the artist

13
Rock and Wave Form
1980s
Alabaster
53 x 19 x 18 cm (21 x 7½ x 7 in.)
Estate of the artist

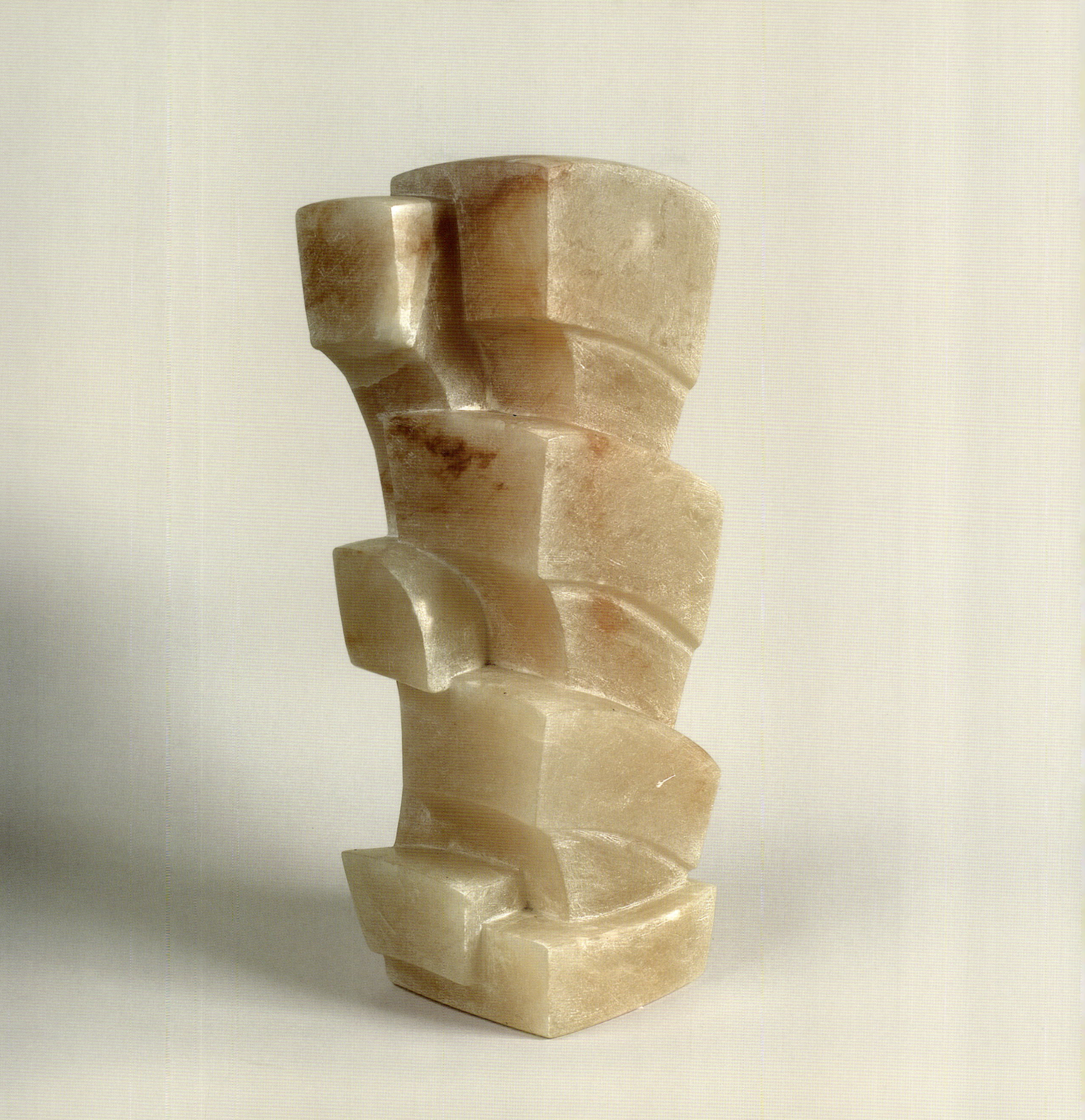

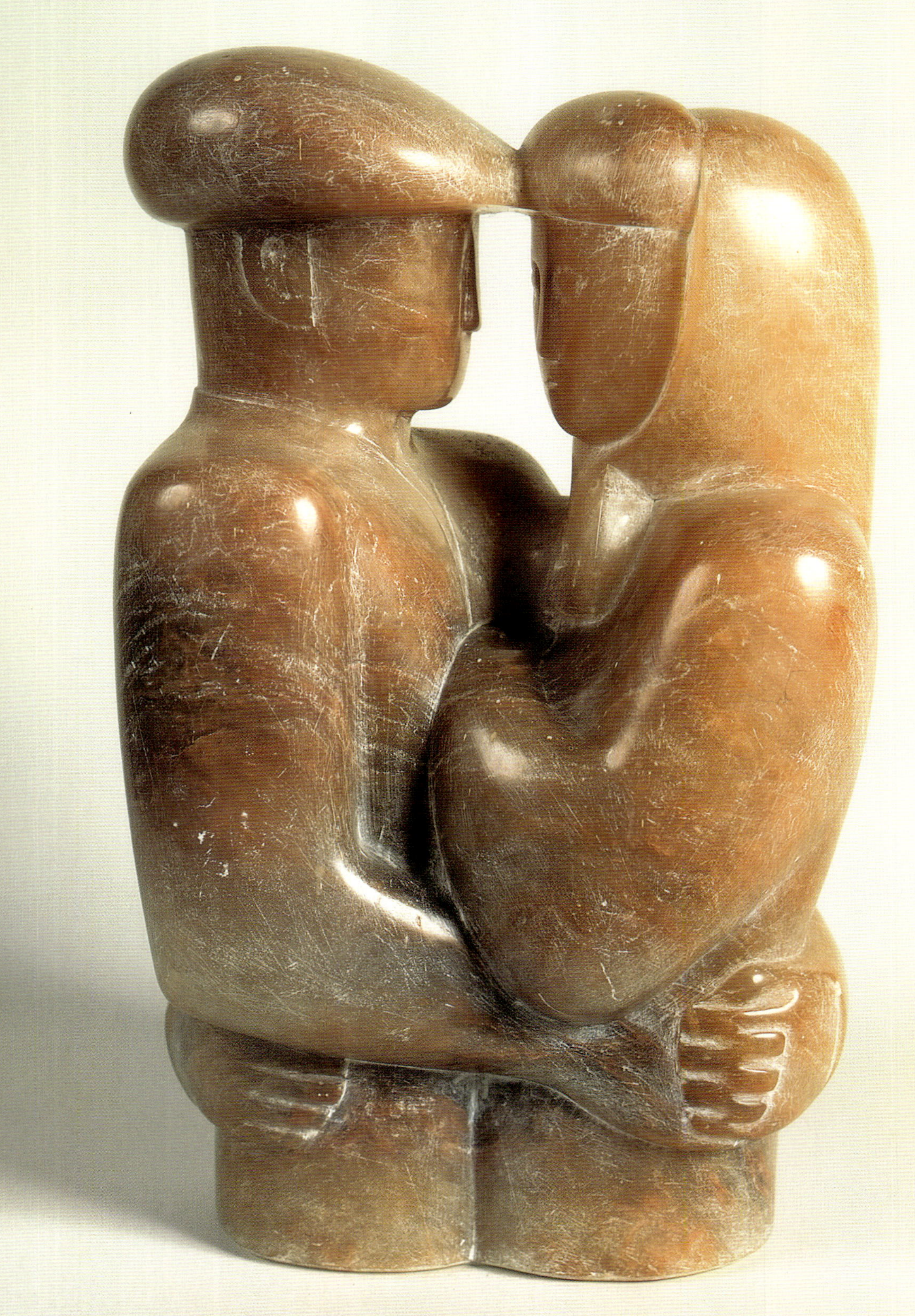

14
Couple
Early 1960s
Alabaster
46 x 25.5 x 20 cm (18 x 10 x 8 in.)
Estate of the artist

15
Reclining Figure
c. 1975
Alabaster
46 x 28 x 21.5 cm (18 x 11 x 8½ in.)
Private collection, Switzerland

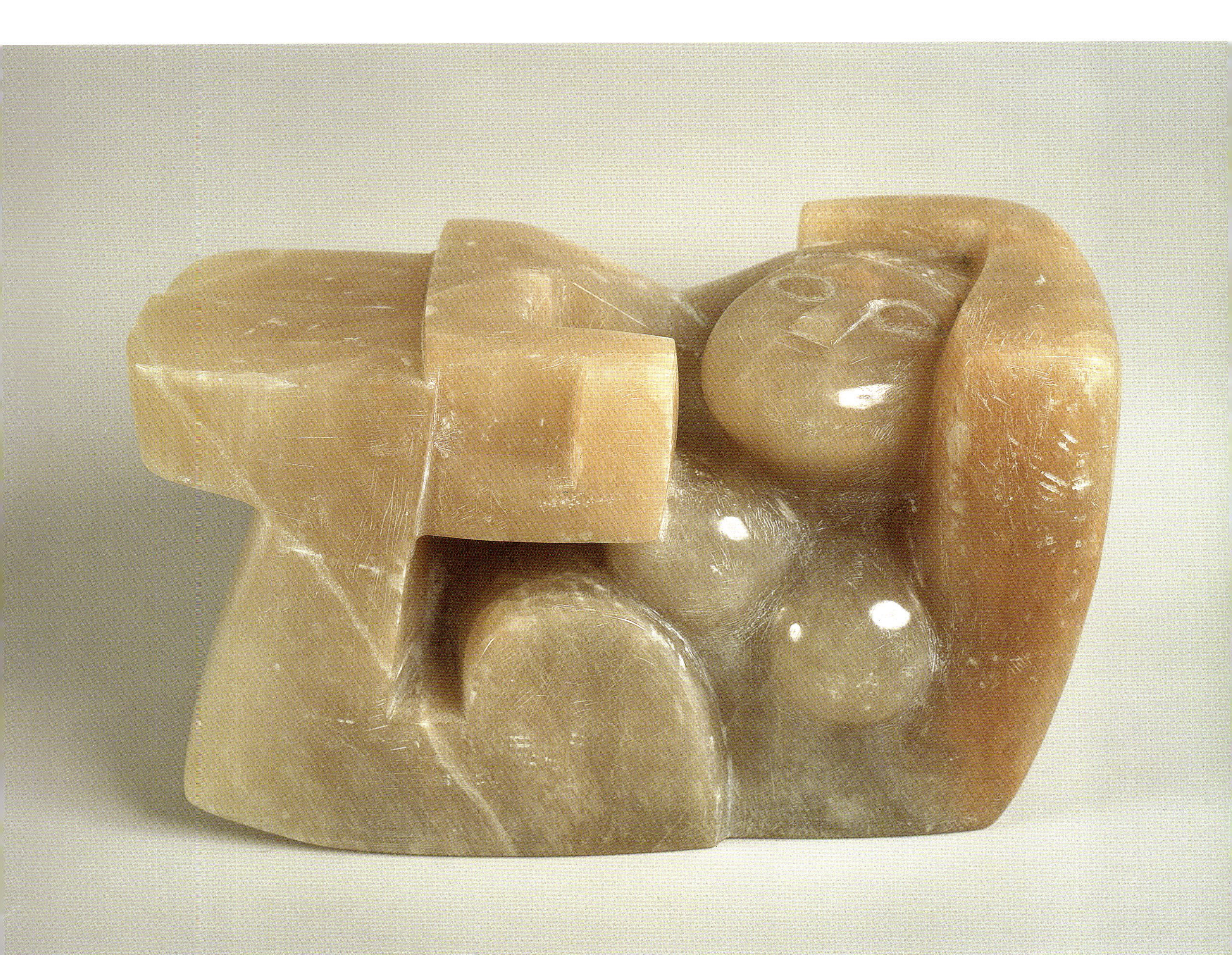

16
Standing Man
1980s
Belgian marble
71 x 24 x 14 cm (28 x 9½ x 5½ in.)
Estate of the artist: reserve collection

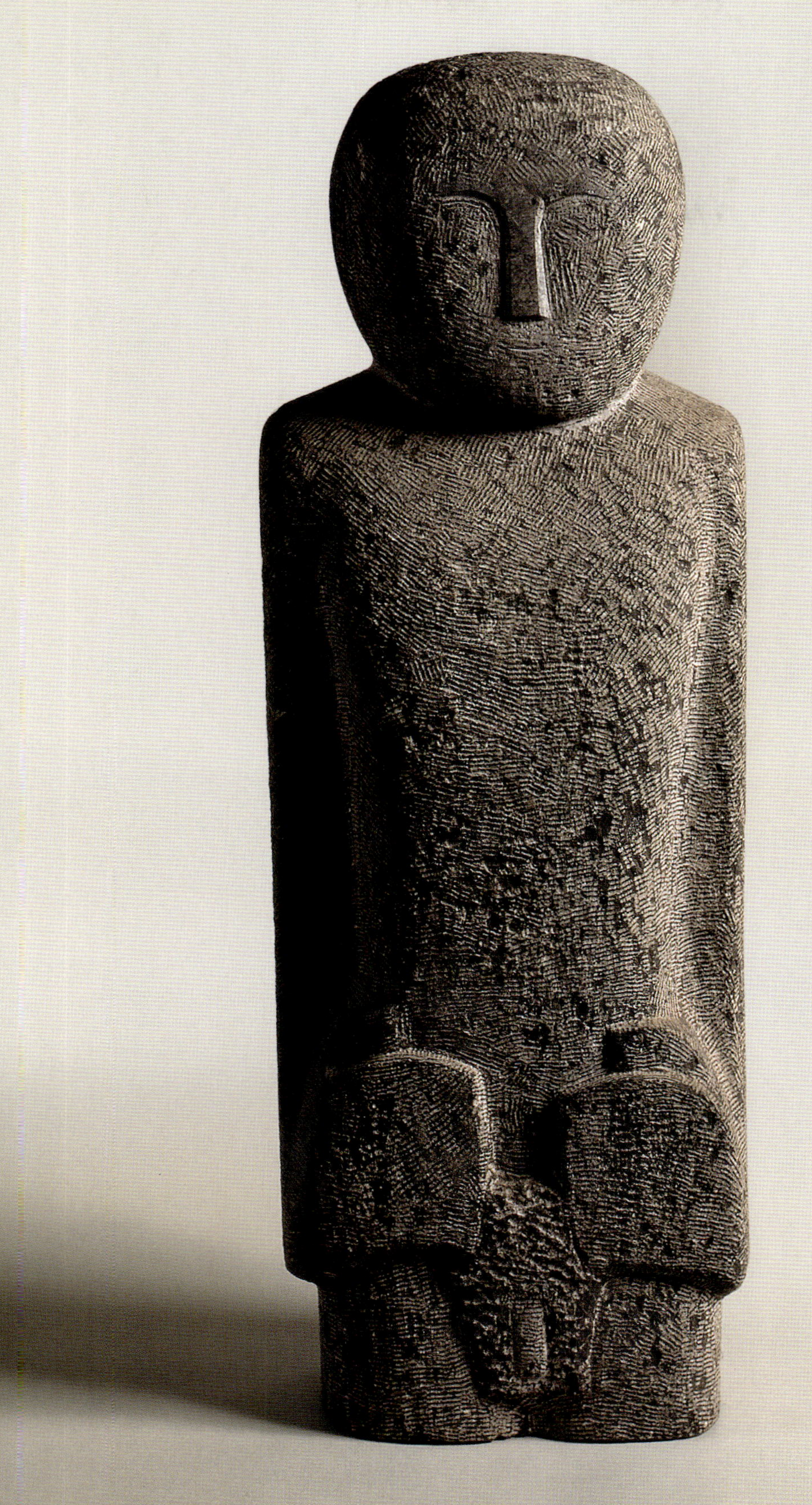

17
Waves
1970–80
Purbeck marble
30.5 x 30.5 x 20 cm (12 x 12 x 8 in.)
Estate of the artist

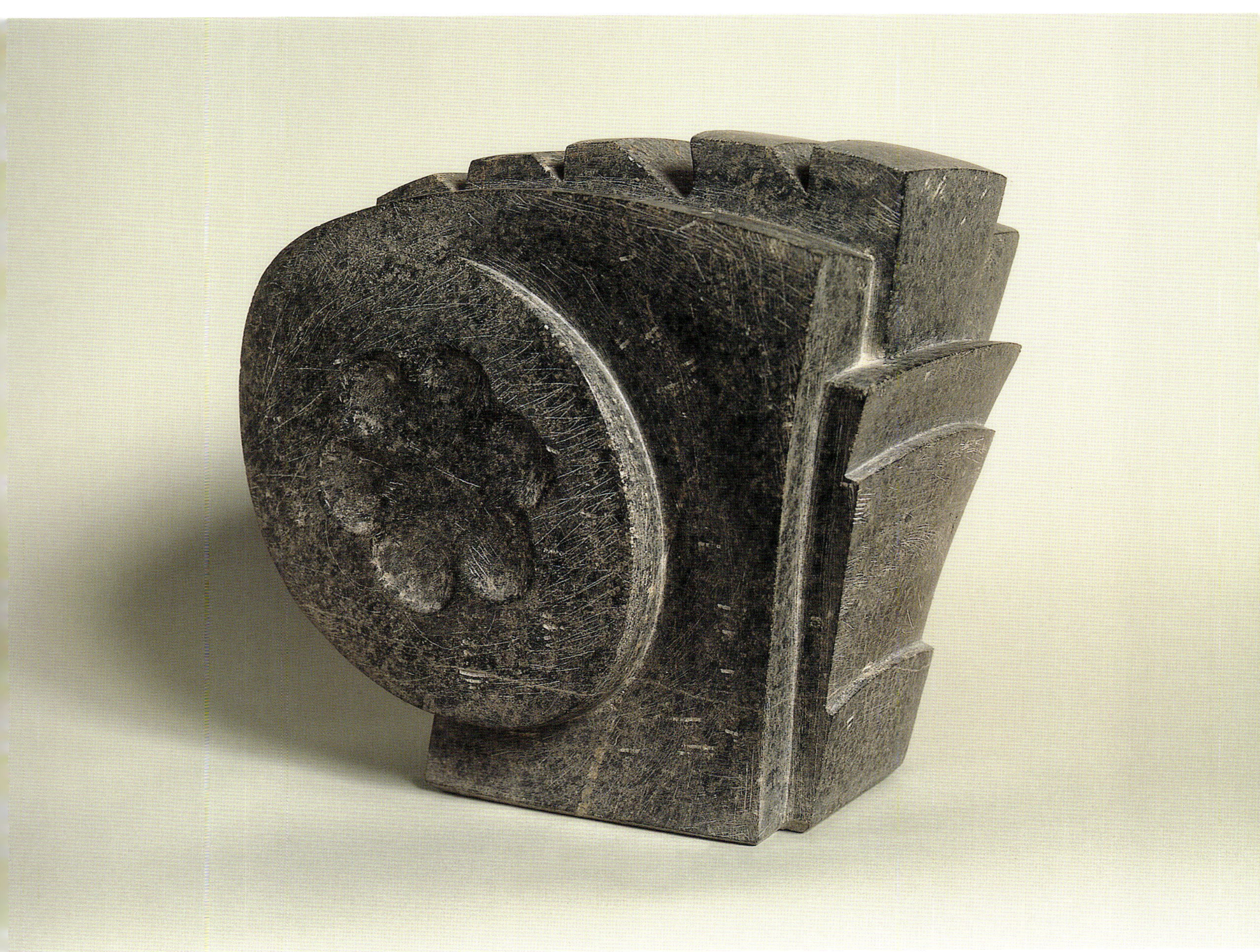

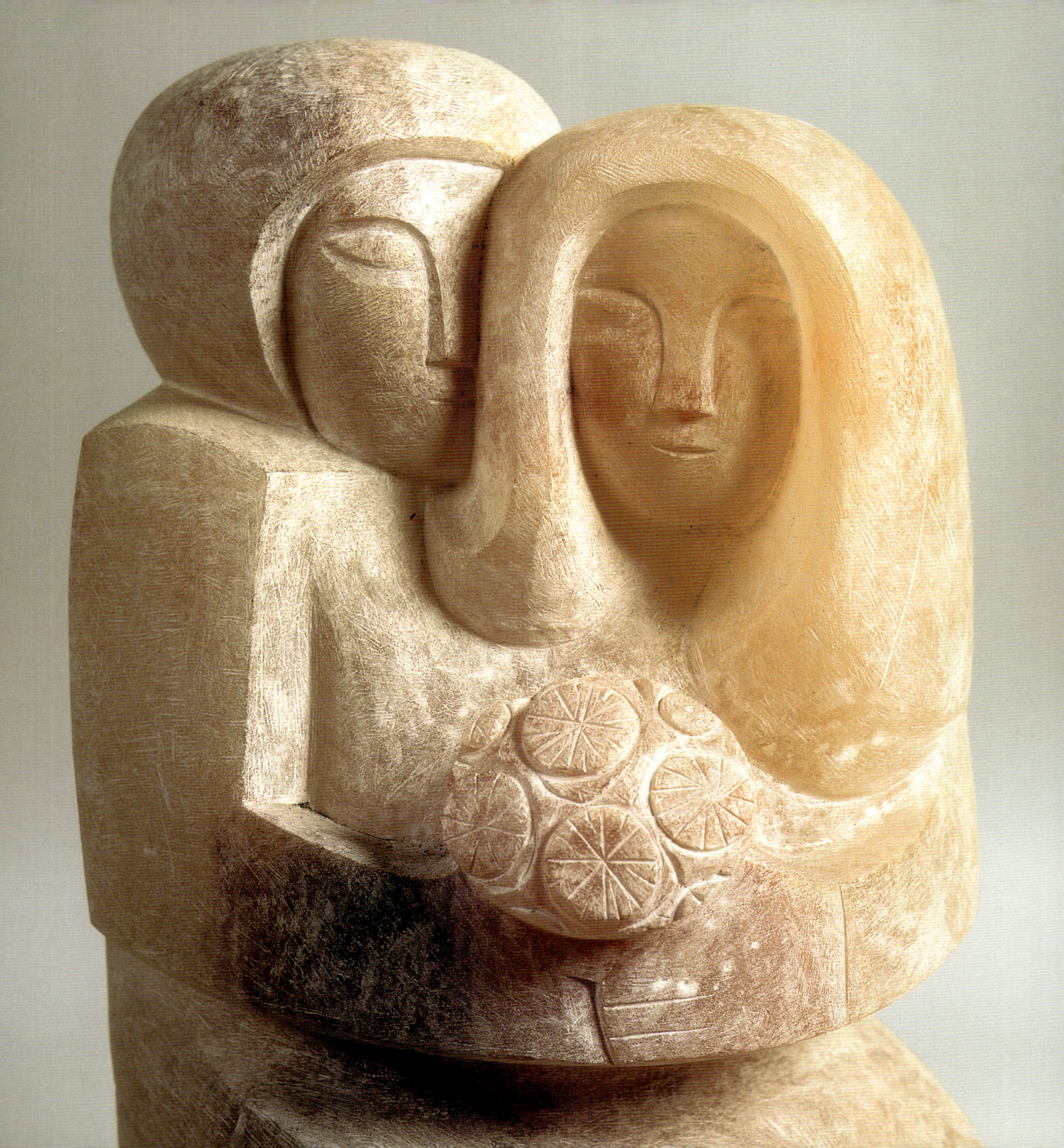

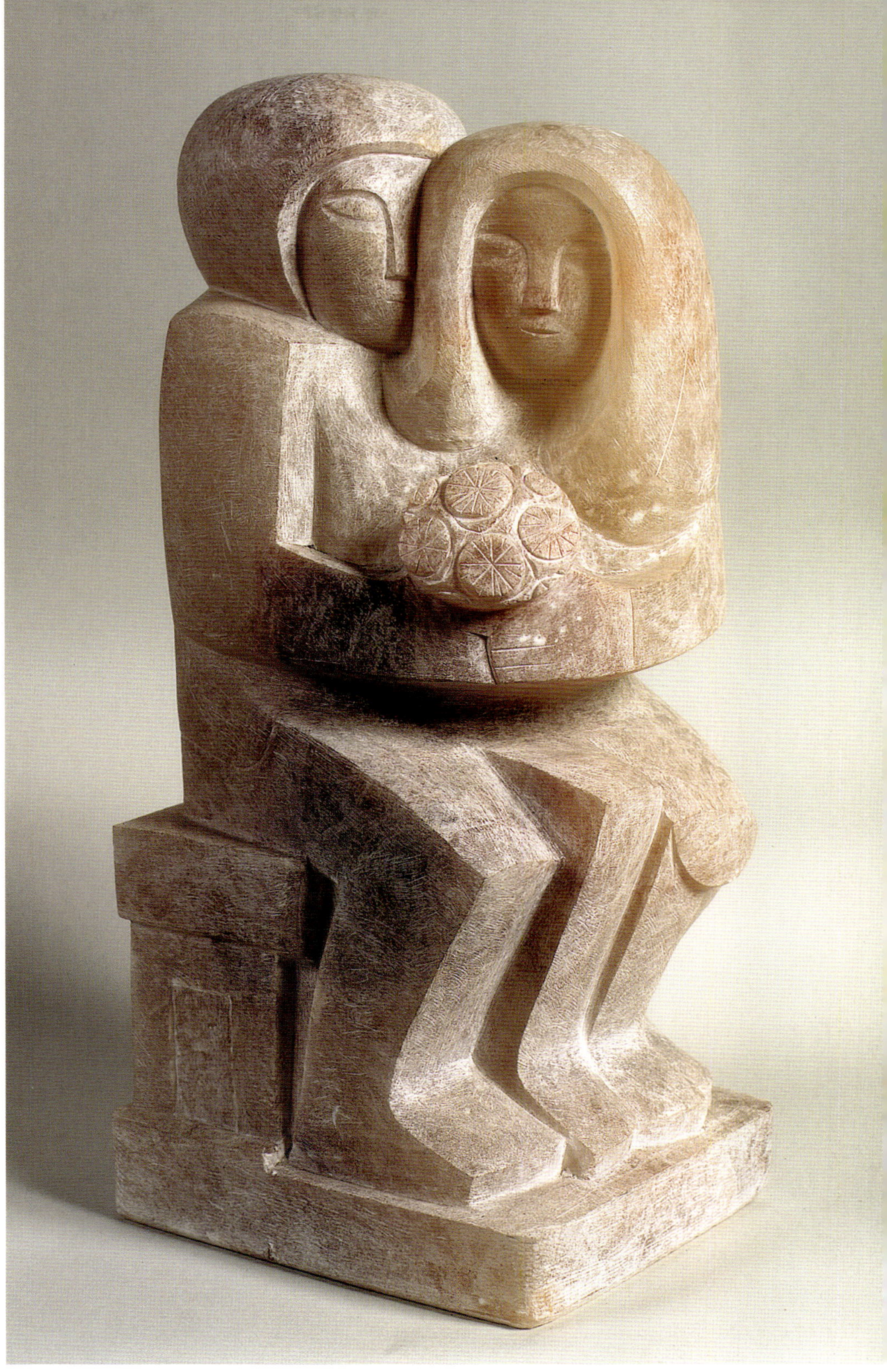

18
Couple with Flowers
1980s
Unpolished alabaster
59.5 x 25.5 x 24 cm (23½ x 10½ x 9½ in.)
Estate of the artist

19
Flower Shape
Late 1960s
Hornton stone
32 x 20 x 20 cm (12½ x 8 x 8 in.)
Estate of the artist

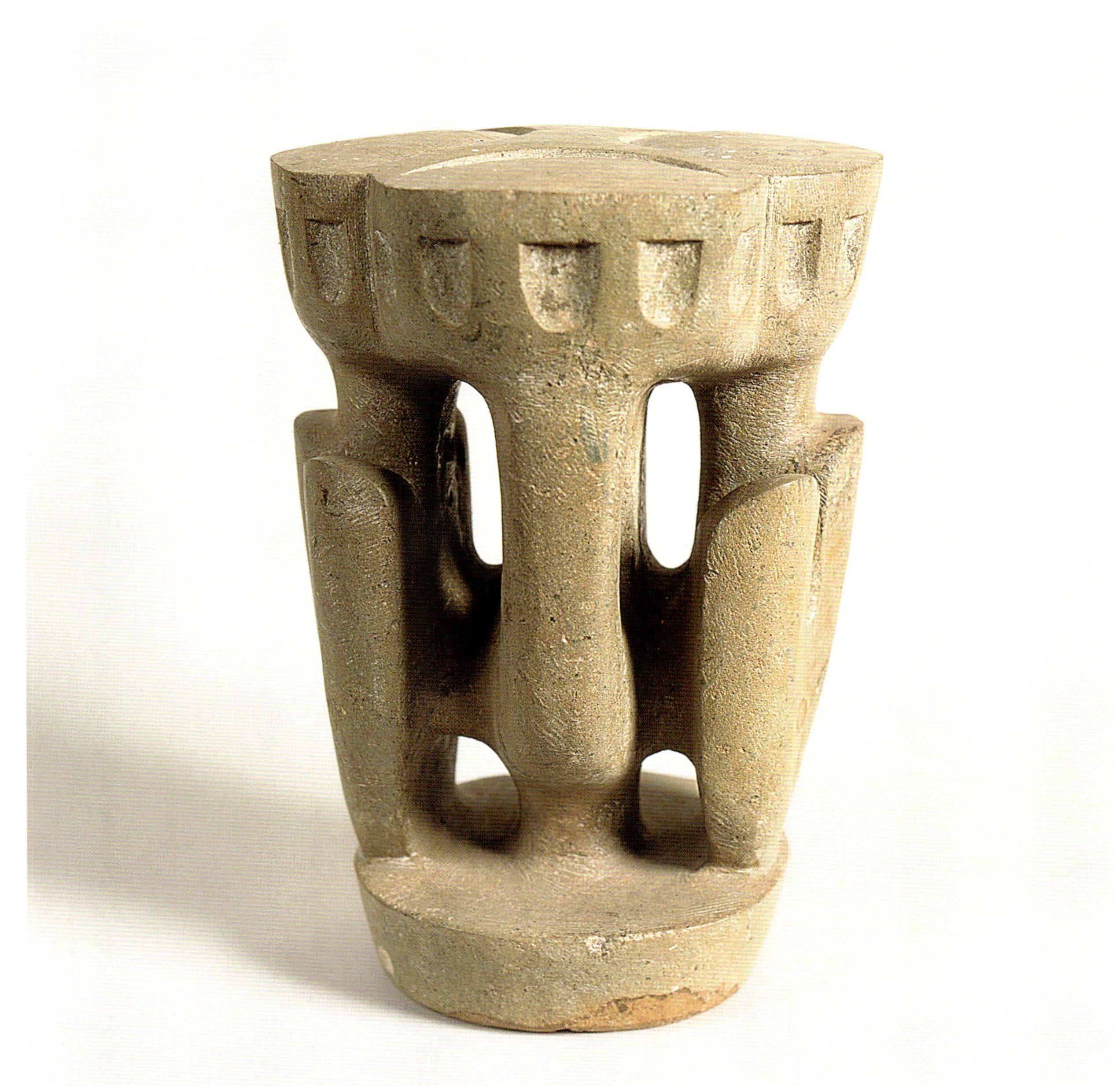

20
Swimmer
1988
Ketton stone
51 x 58.5 x 9 cm (20 x 23 x 3½ in.)
Estate of the artist

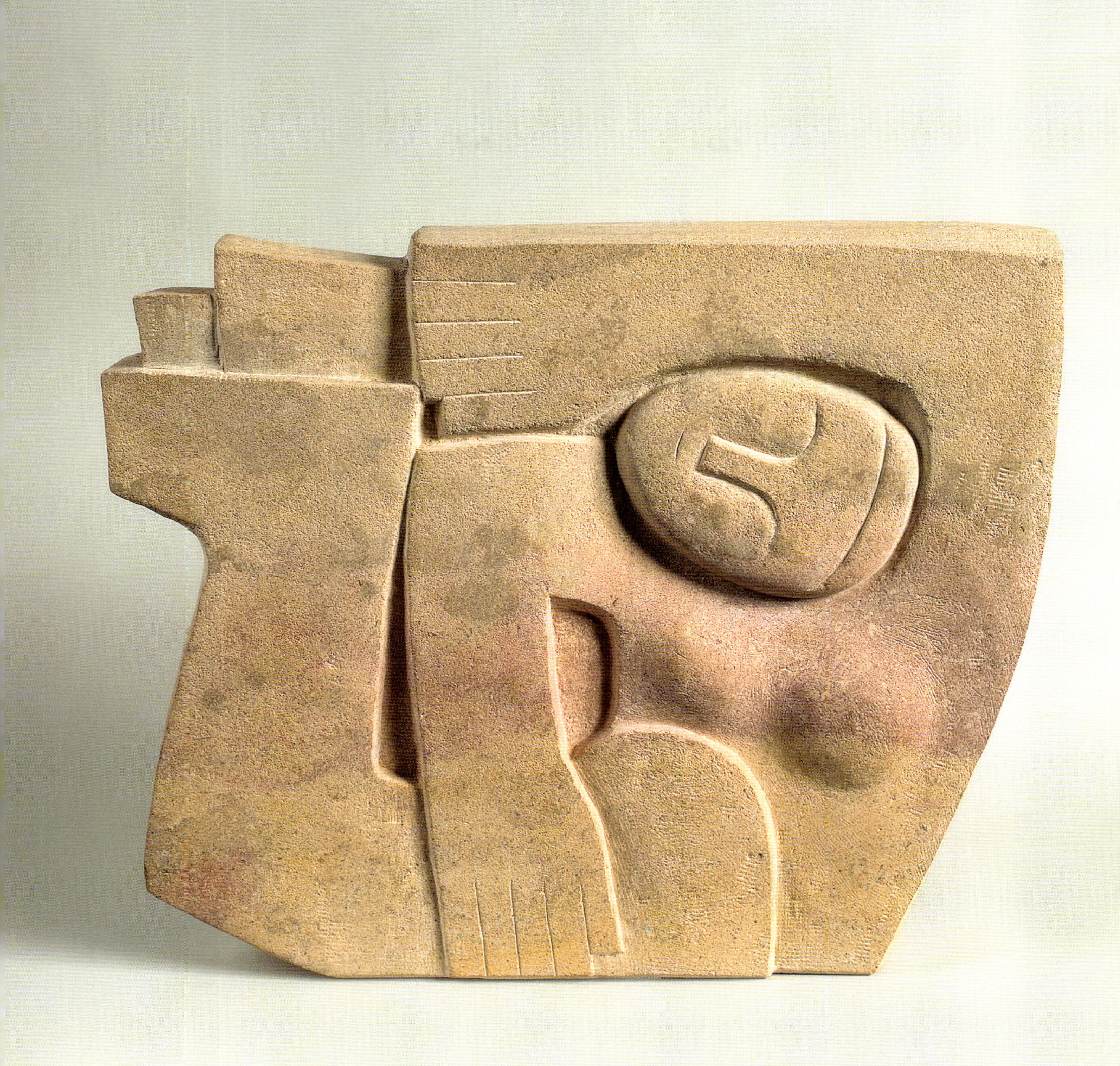

21
Seated Figure
1965–75
Alabaster
71 x 29 x 34 cm (28 x 11½ x 13½ in.)
Estate of the artist: reserve collection

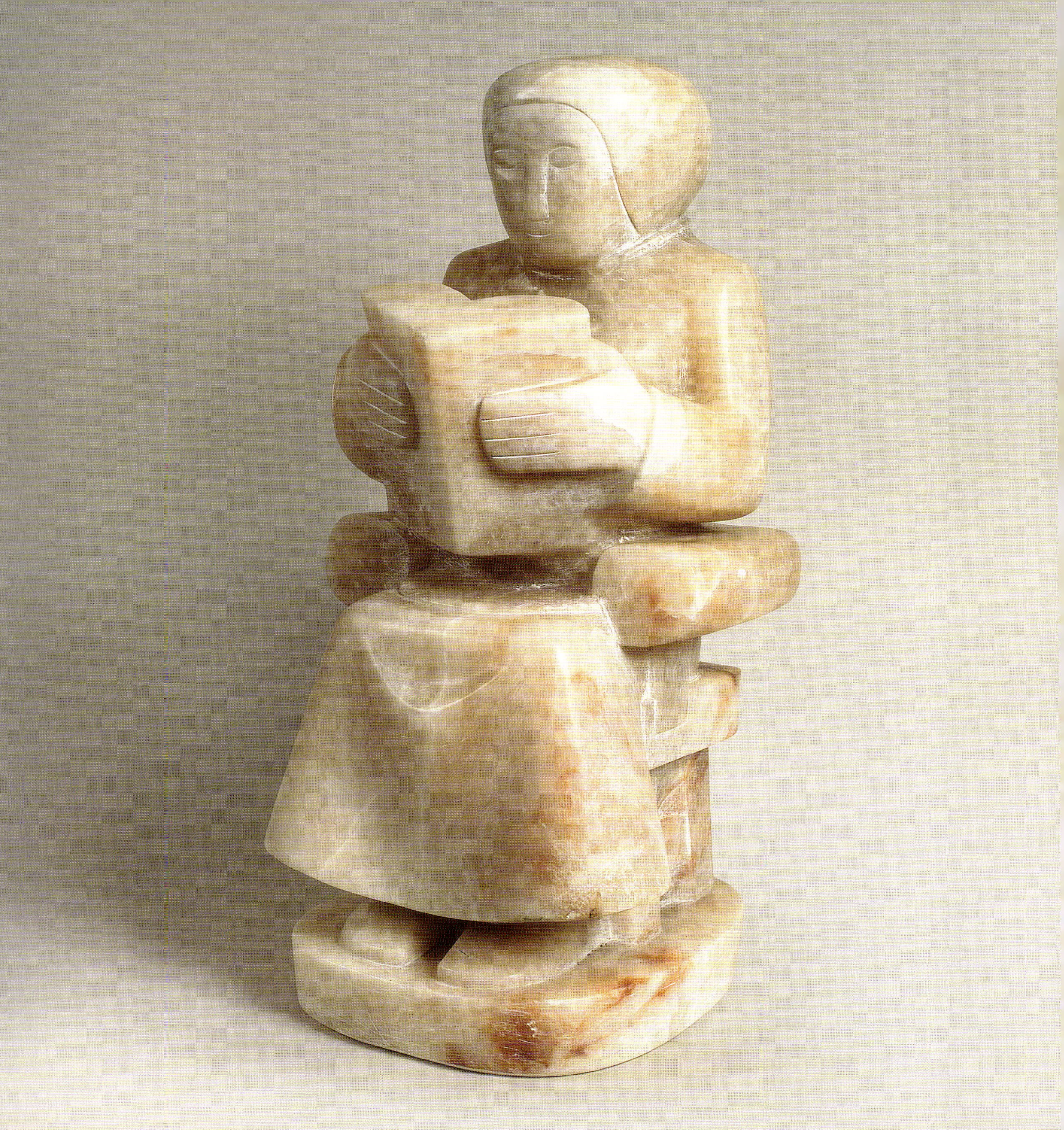

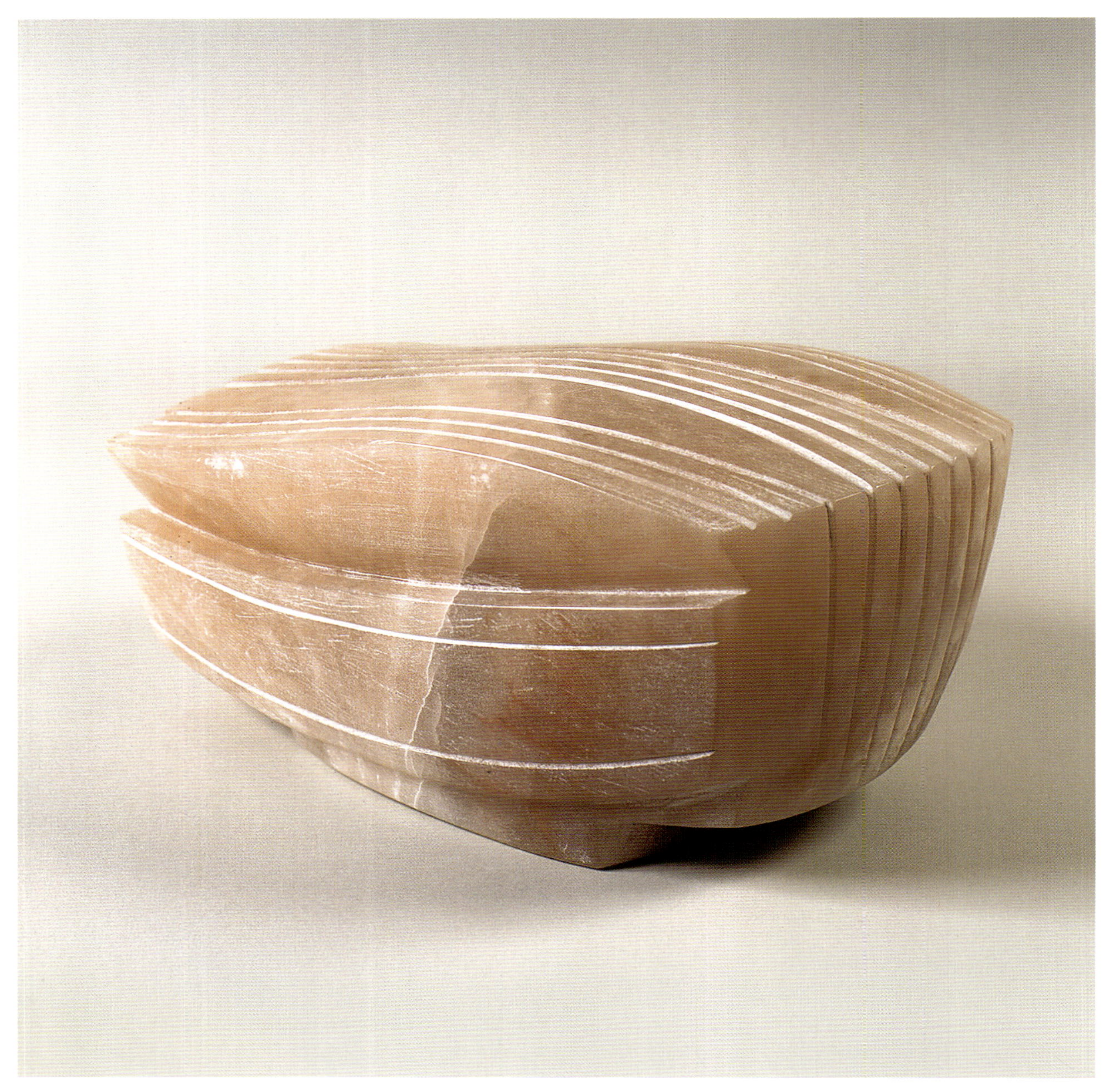

22
Crystal Stream
1980s
Alabaster
20 x 38 x 25.5 cm (8 x 15 x 10 in.)
Estate of the artist: reserve collection

23
Traveller (*Boy with Bird on his Shoulder*)
1980s
Brown Hornton stone
66 x 30.5 x 19 cm (26 x 12 x 7½ in.)
Estate of the artist

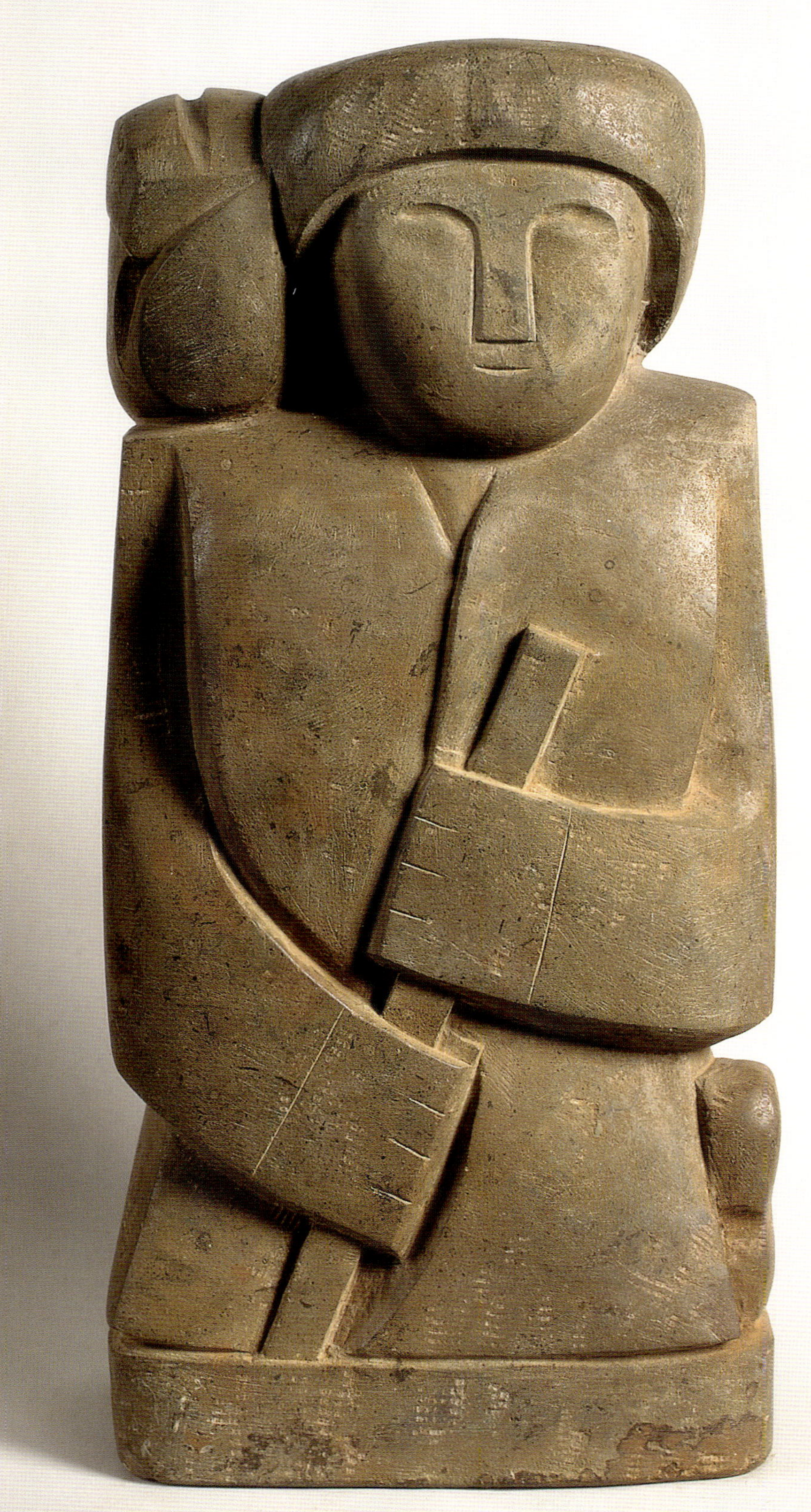

24
Girl
1980s
Alabaster
53 x 23 x 15 cm (21 x 9 x 6 in.)
Estate of the artist

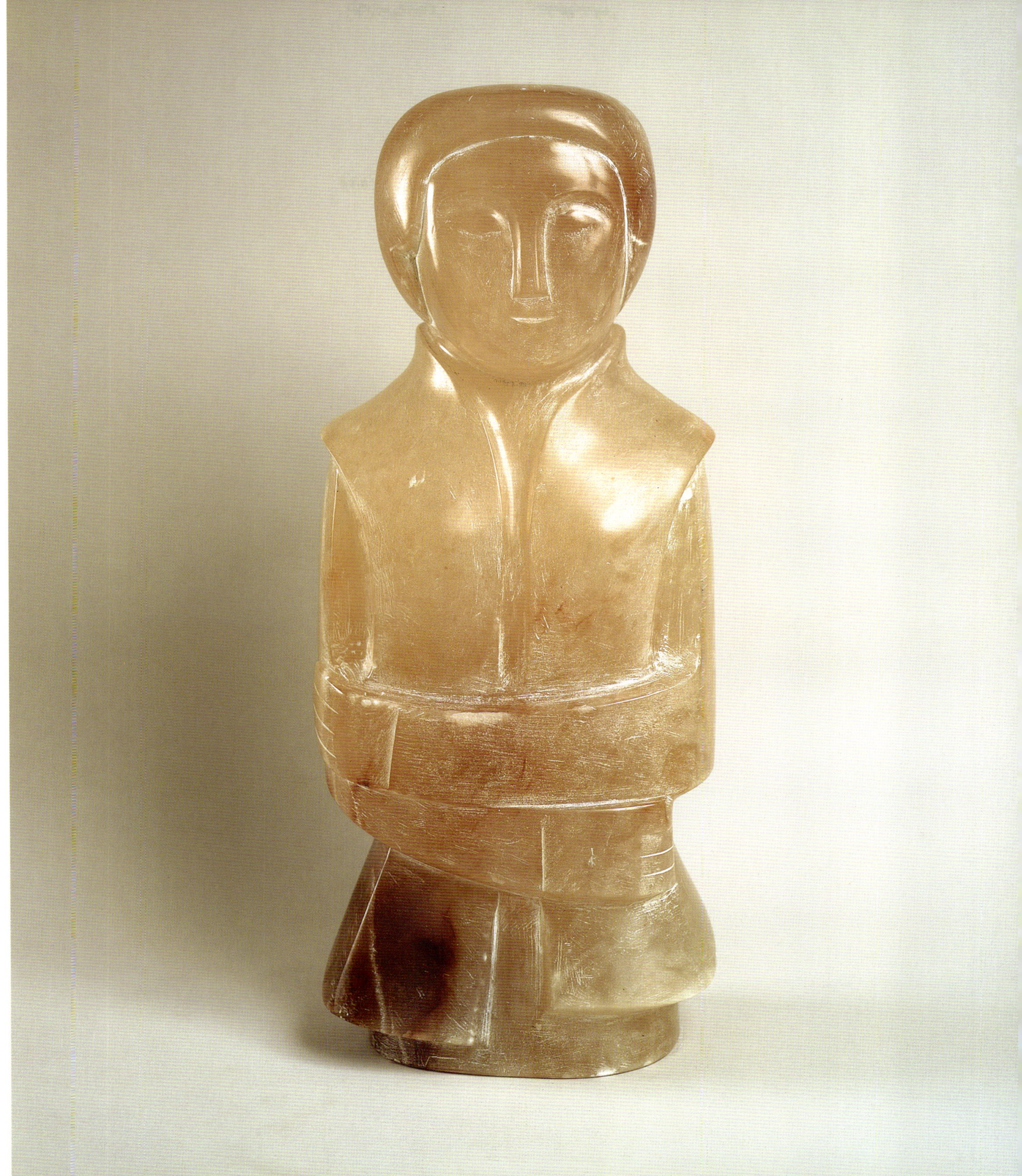

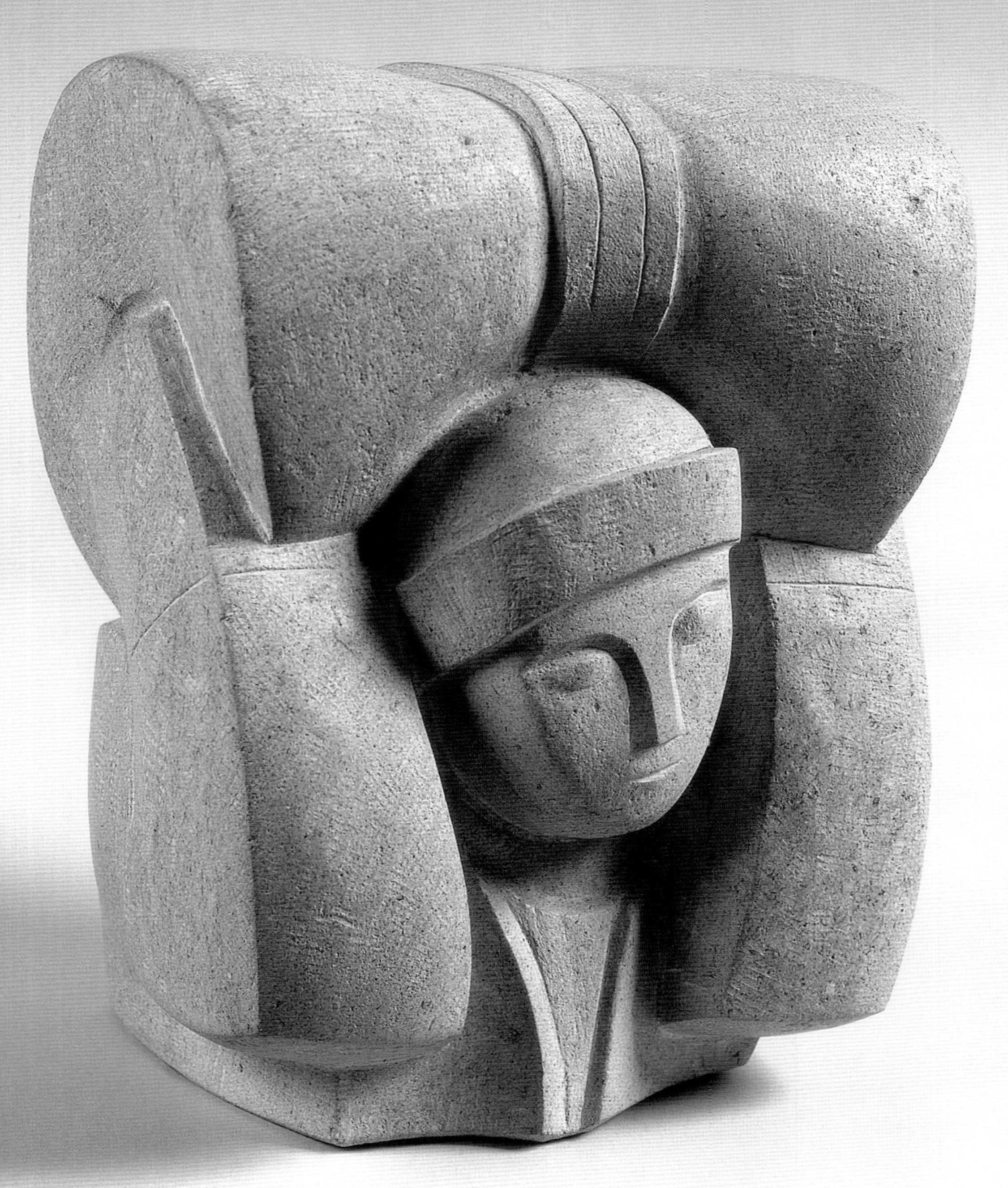

25
Man with a Mattress
c. 1985
Clipsham stone
40.5 x 30.5 x 21.5 cm (16 x 12 x 8½ in.)
Estate of the artist: reserve collection

26
Landscape with Sun
1970–80
Clipsham stone
35.5 x 48 x 15 cm (14 x 19 x 6 in.)
Estate of the artist

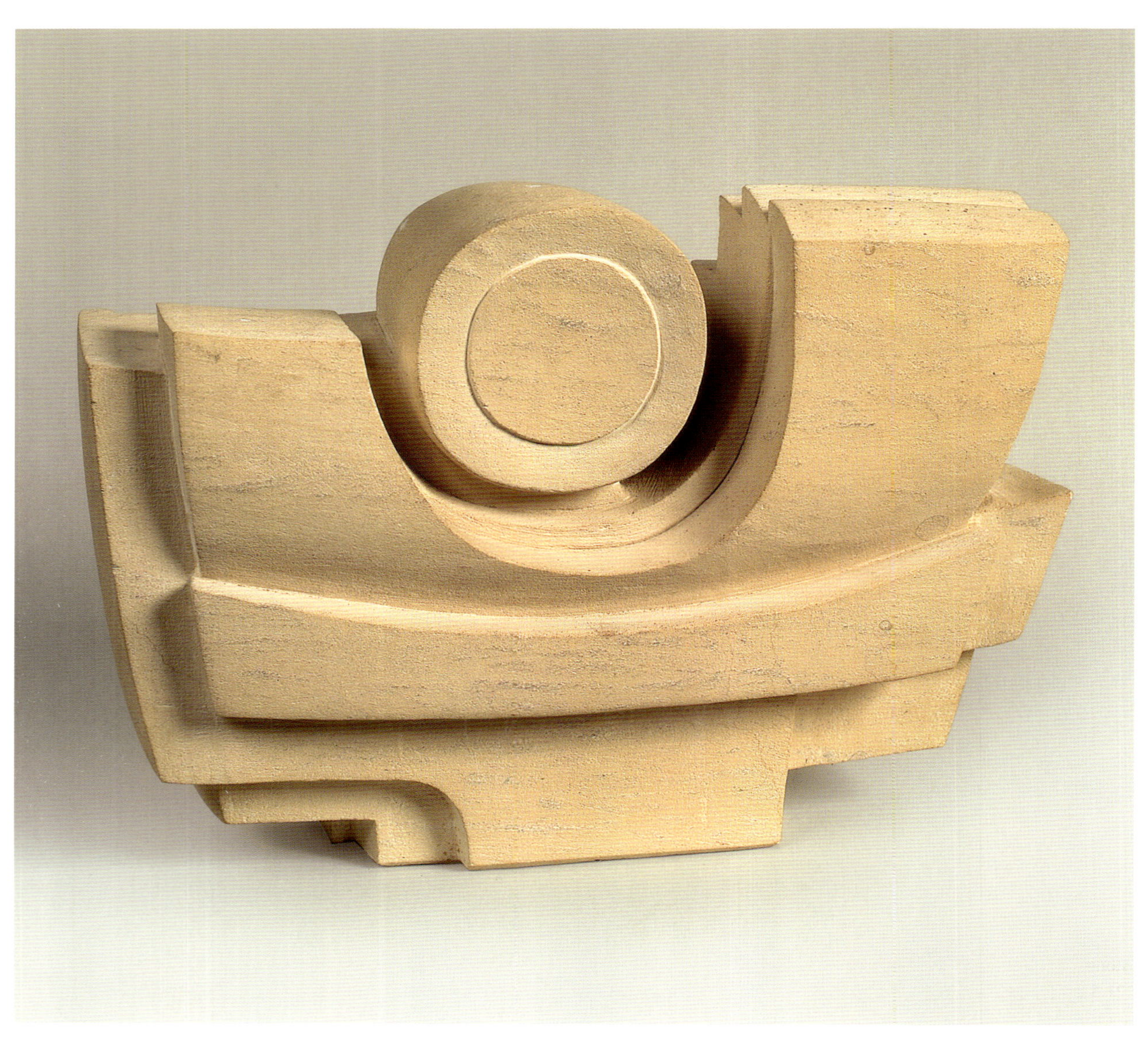

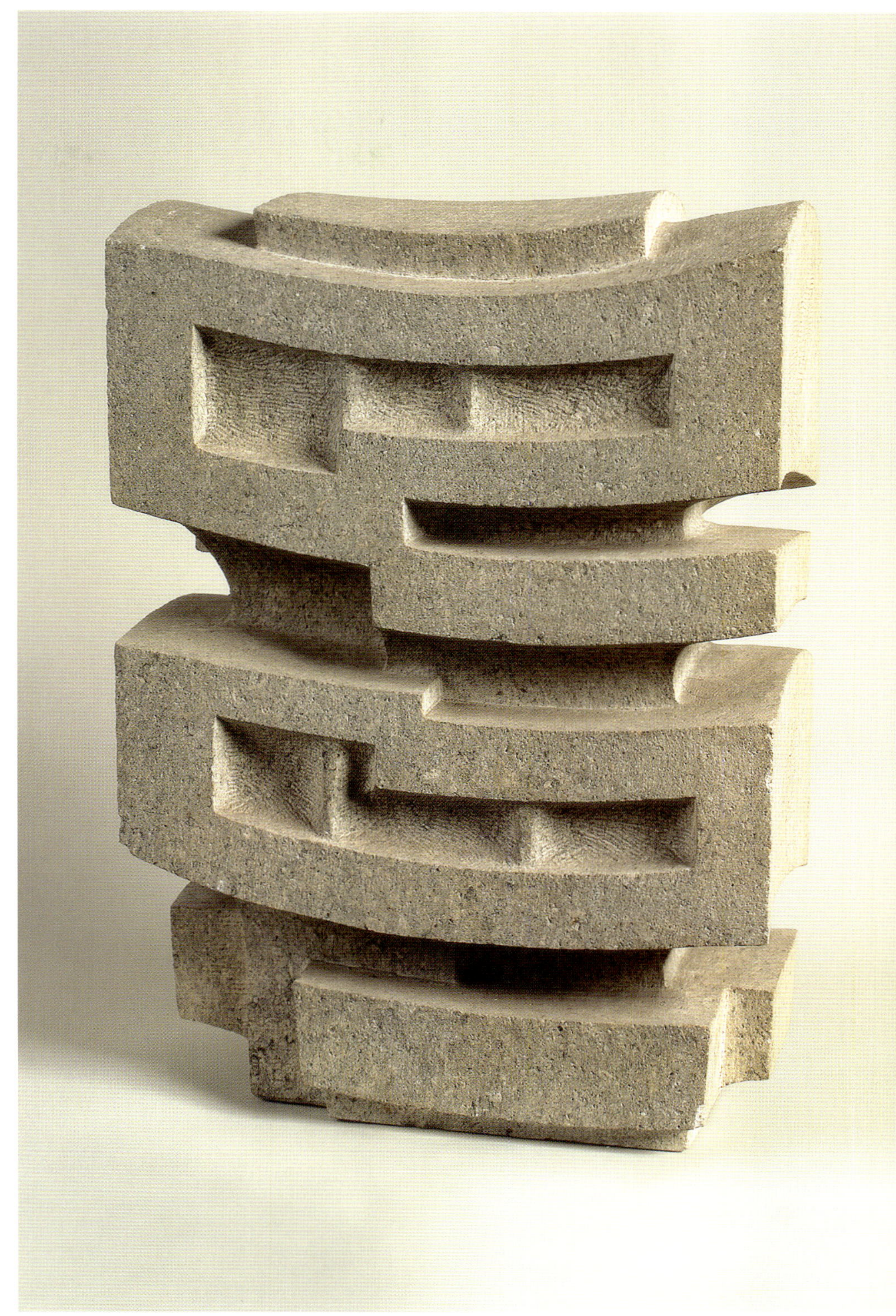

27
Sea Piece
1980s
Clipsham stone
57 x 38 x 21.5 cm (22½ x 15 x 8½ in.)
Estate of the artist

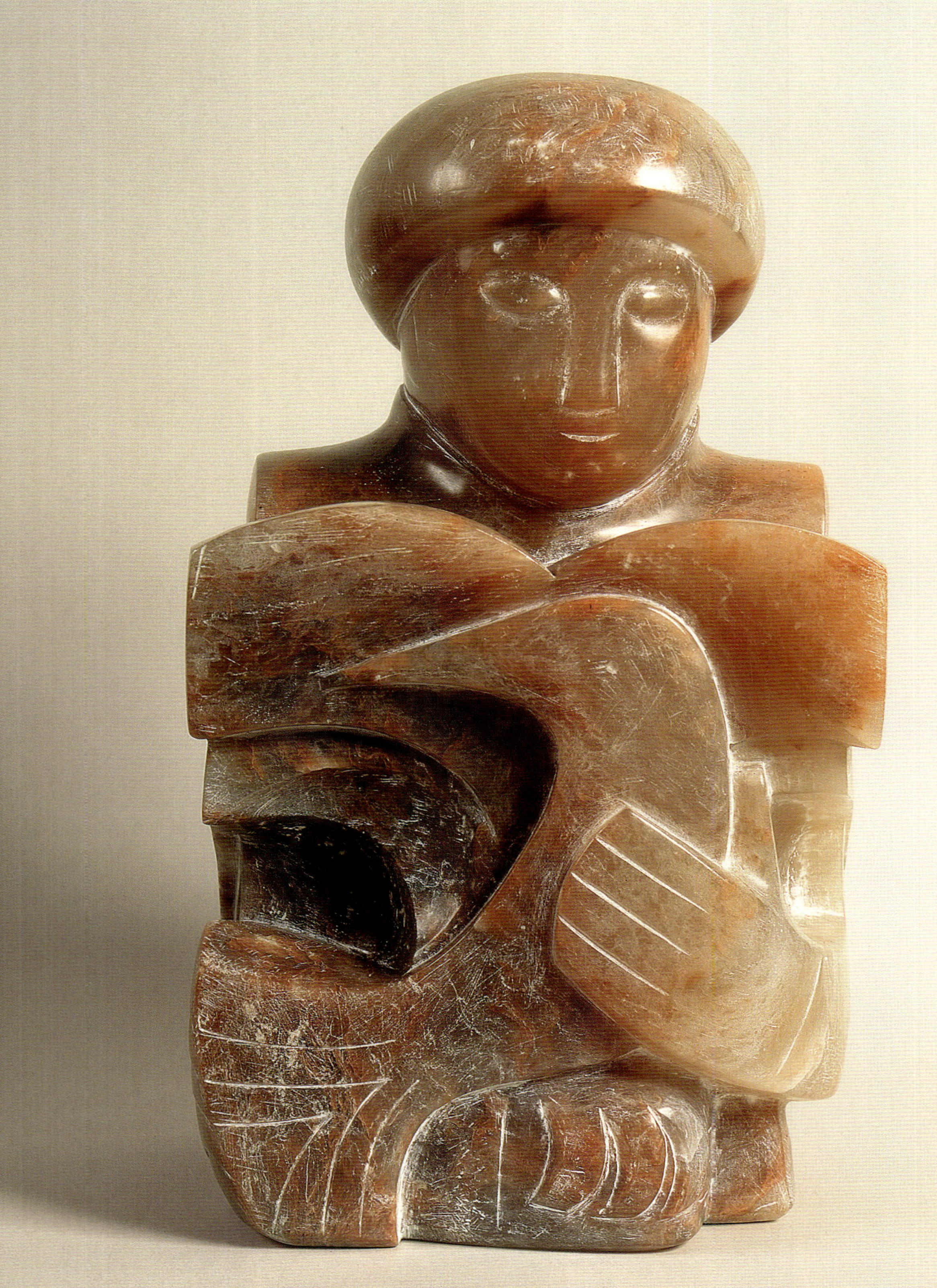

28
Boy with a Bird
1980s
Alabaster
48 x 28 x 20 cm (19 x 11 x 8 in.)
Estate of the artist

29
Reclining Figure
Late 1970s
Clipsham stone
53 x 76 x 13 cm (21 x 30 x 5¼ in.)
Estate of the artist

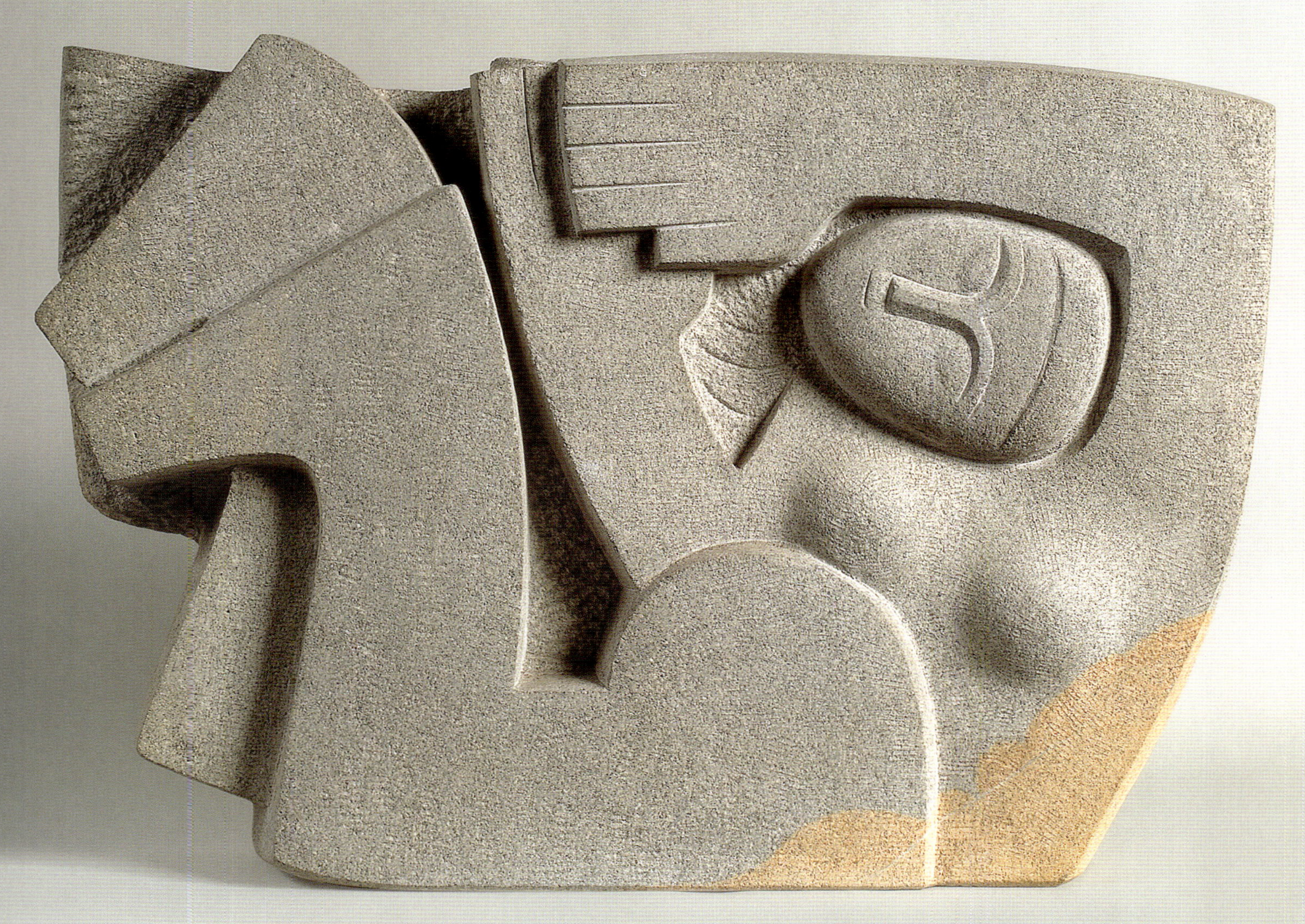

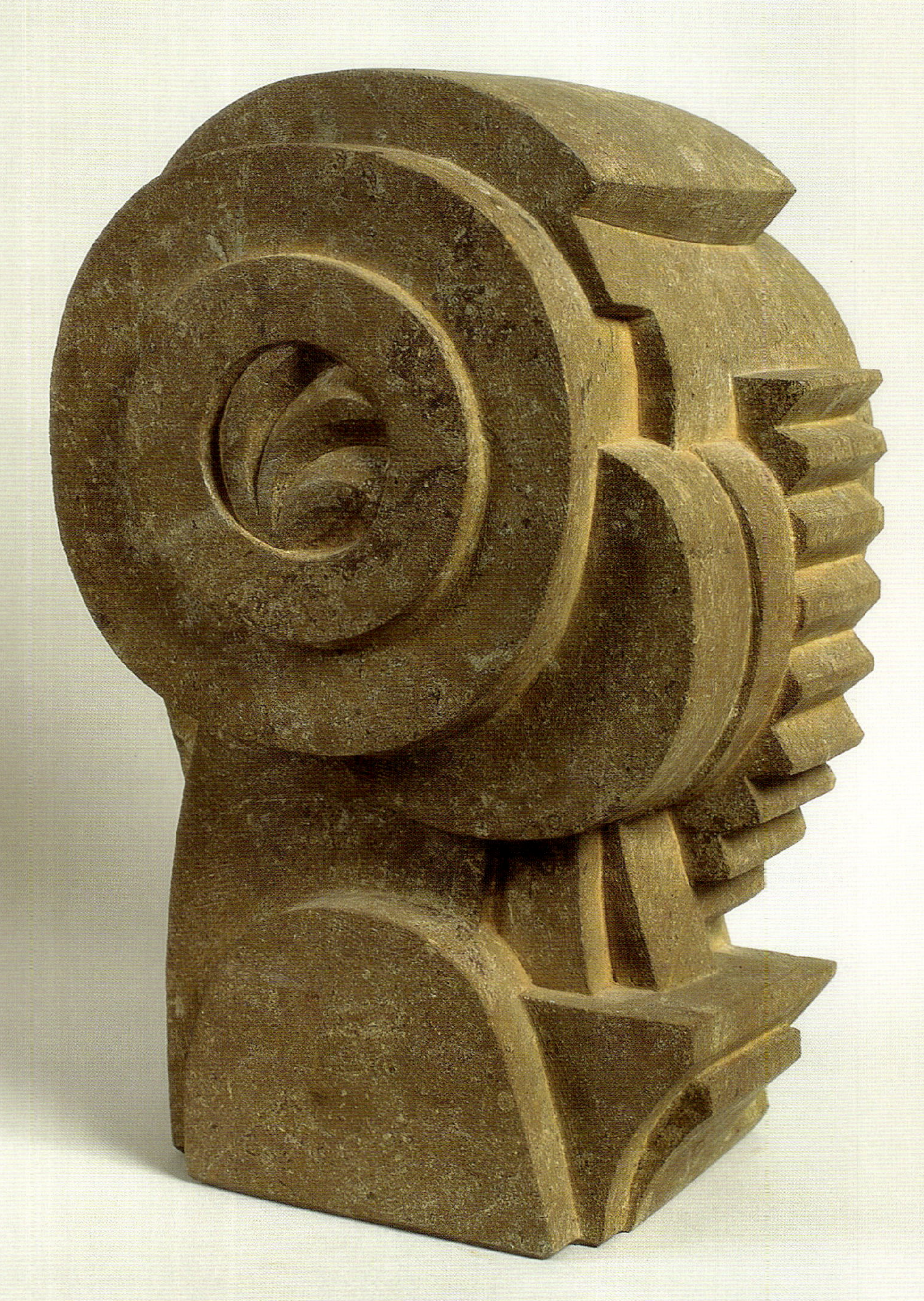

30
Wave
1970s
Brown Hornton stone
42 x 23 x 20 cm (16½ x 9 x 8 in.)
Cantelo Ellis collection, London

31
Crayfish
1970s
Alabaster
35.5 x 48 x 32 cm (14 x 19 x 12½ in.)
Collection Eileen Mackenzie

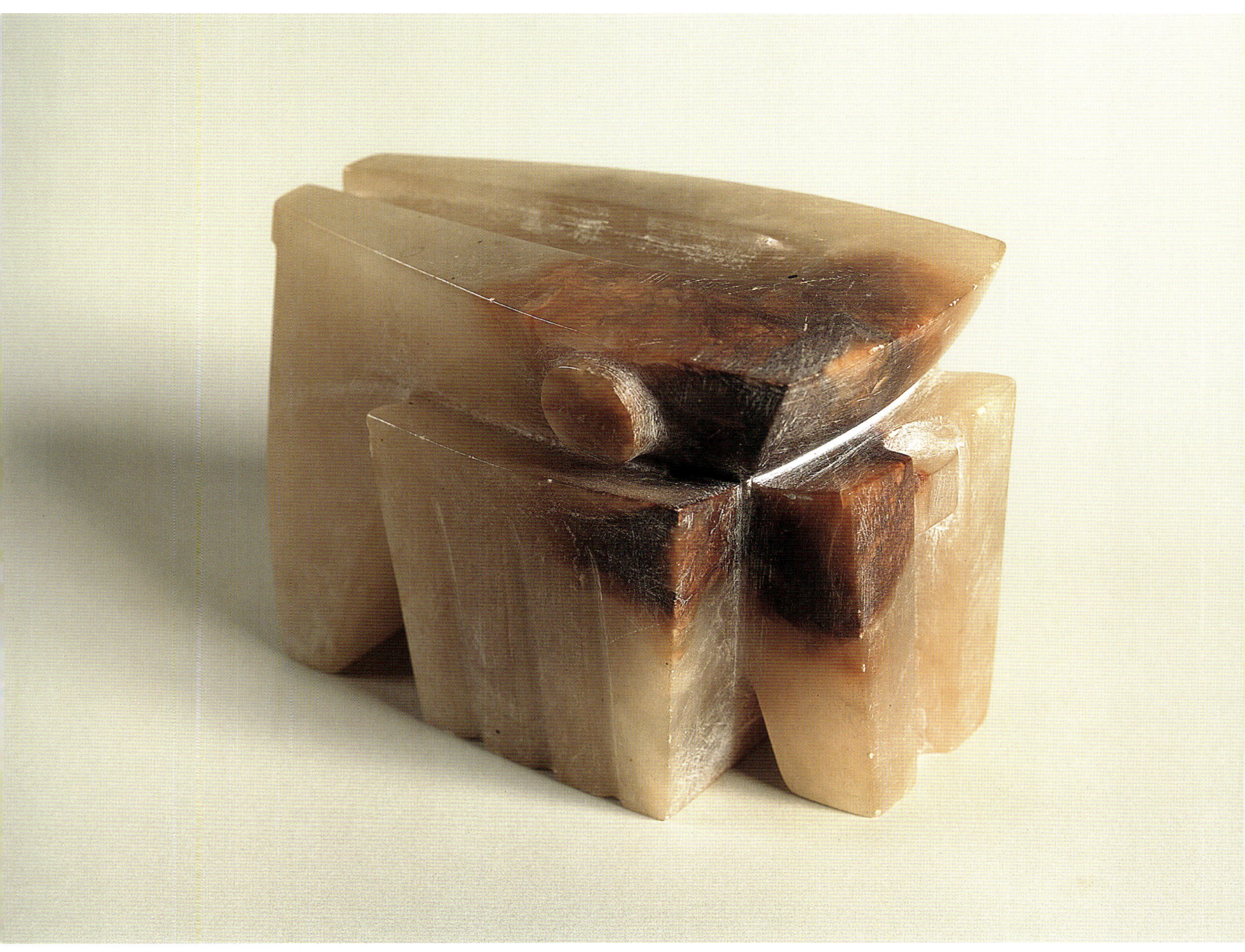

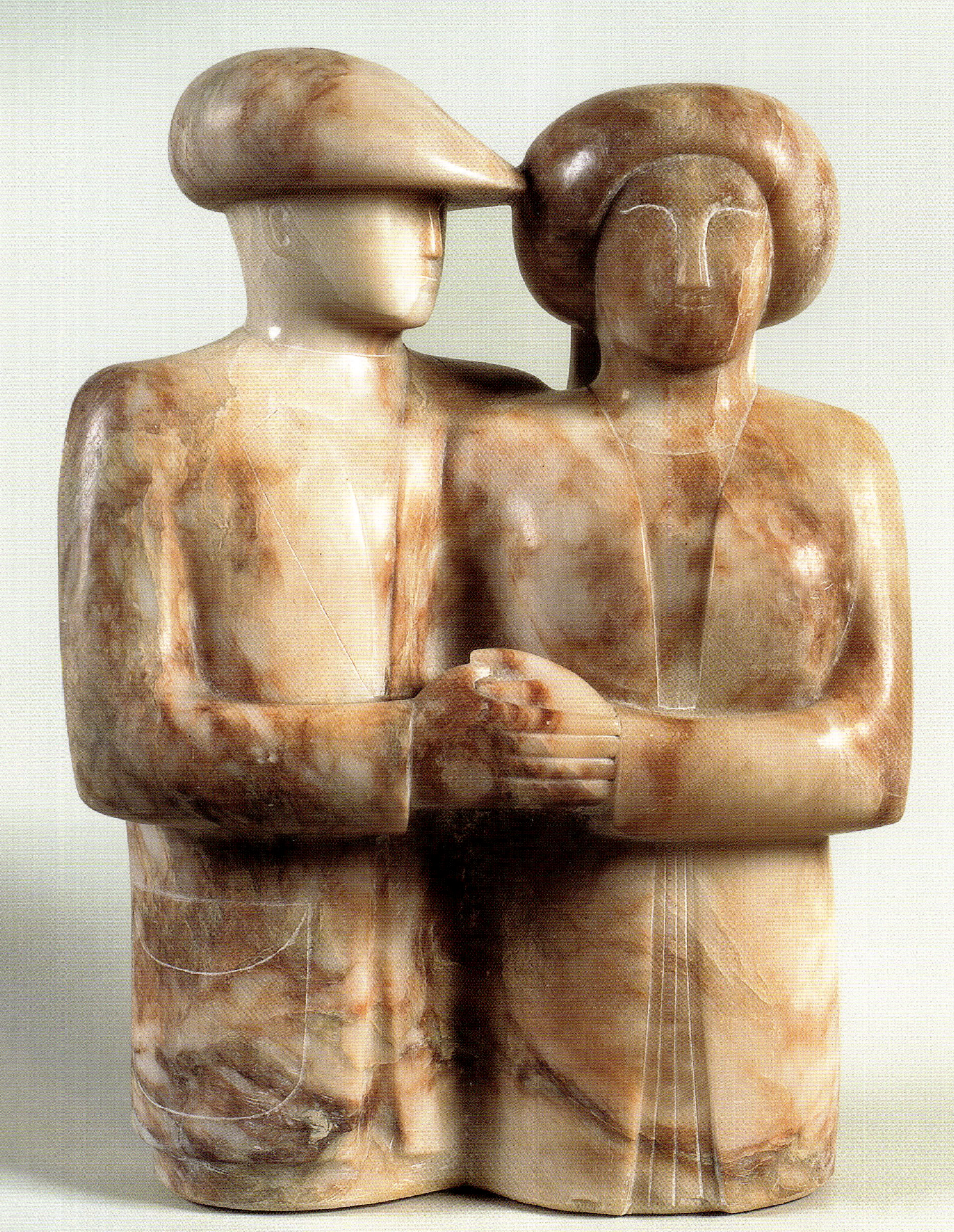

32
Couple
1965–70
Alabaster
63.5 x 44.5 x 21.5 cm (25 x 17½ x 8½ in.)
Estate of the artist: reserve collection

33
Bird, Sunflower
1980s
Alabaster
37 x 30.5 x 15 cm (14½ x 12 x 6 in.)
Estate of the artist

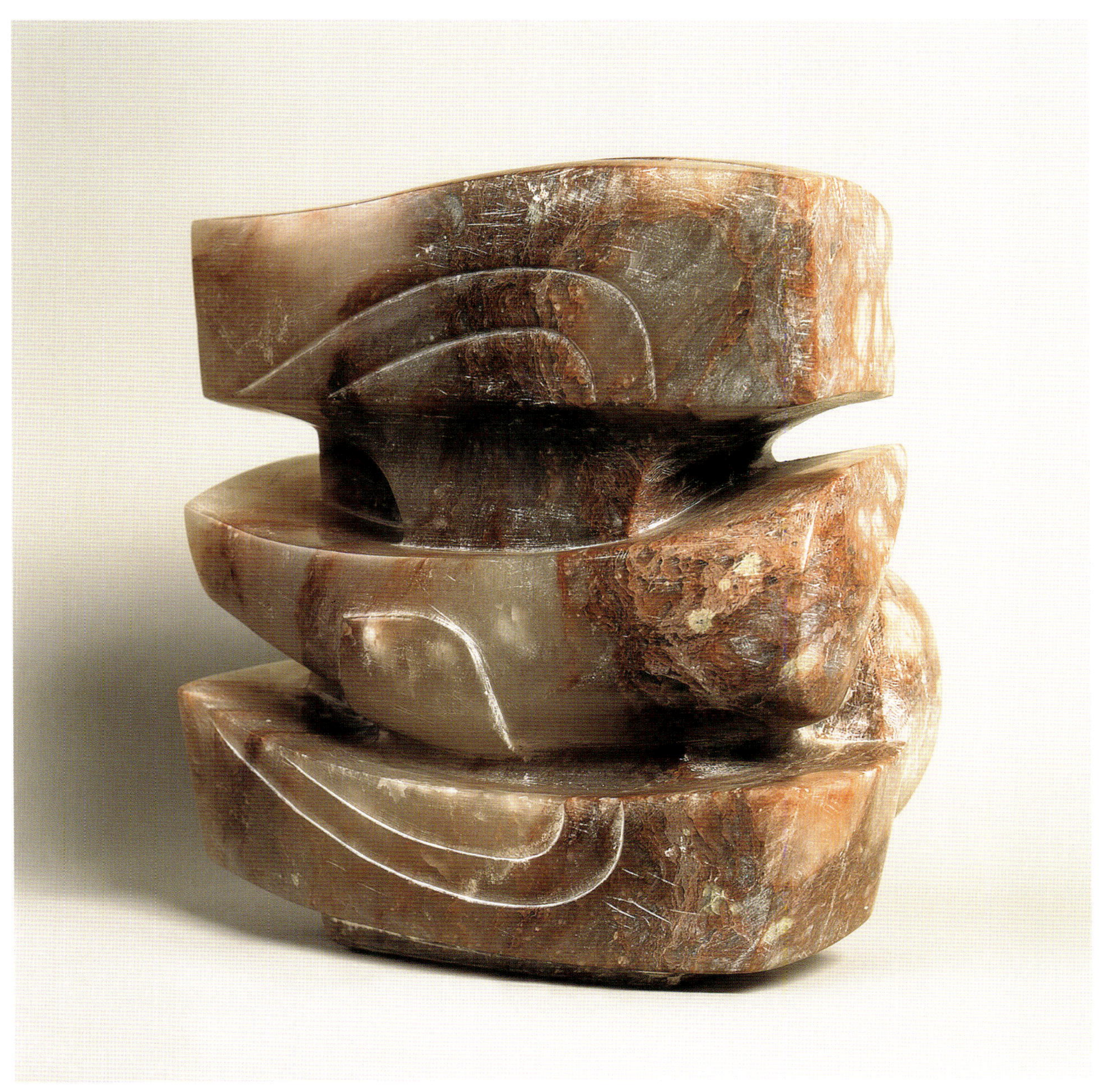

34
Dancing Figure
1965–68
Clipsham stone
91.5 x 28 x 23 cm (36 x 11 x 9 in.)
Estate of the artist: reserve collection

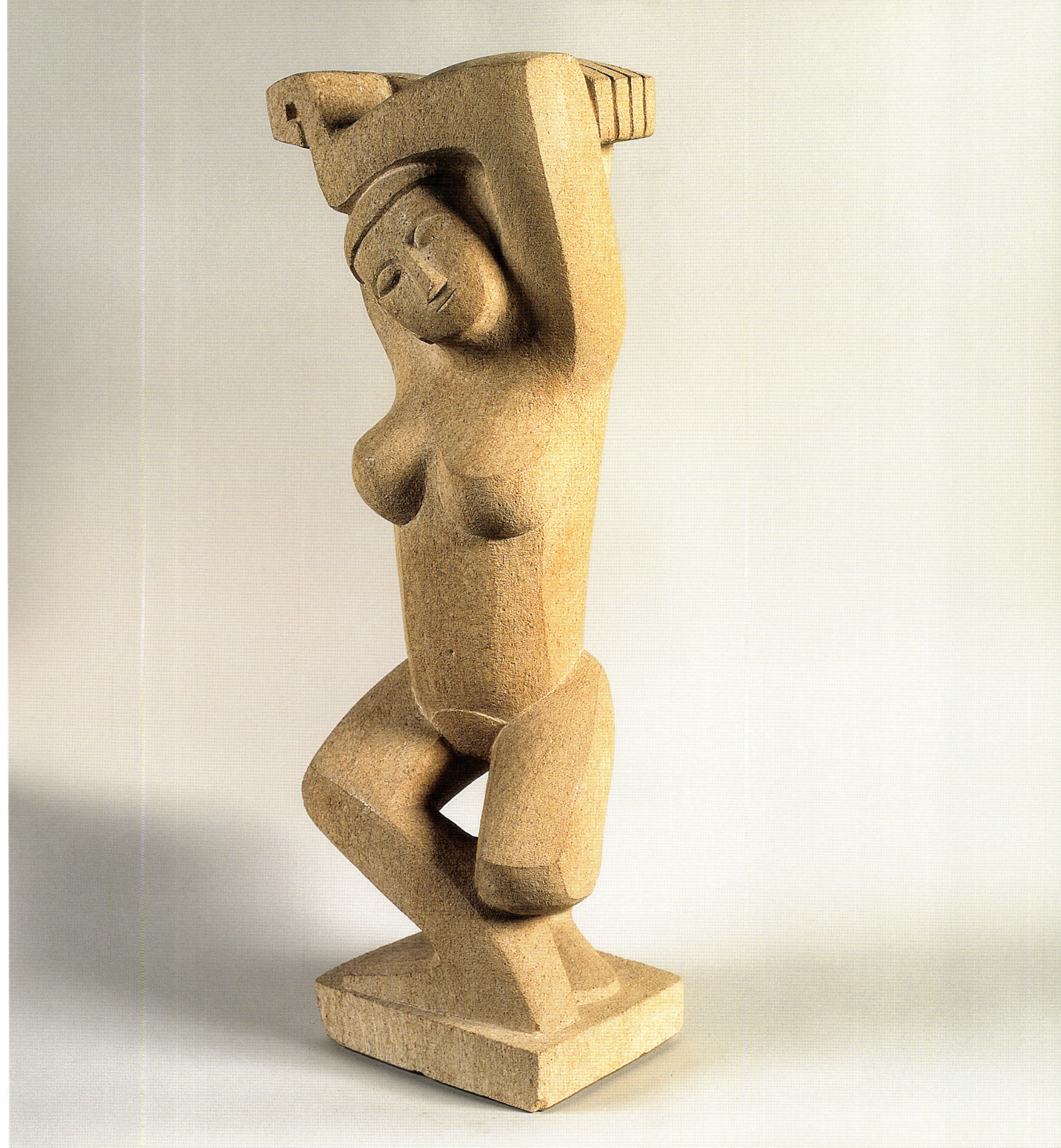

BIOGRAPHY/EXHIBITIONS

1910	Born in Richmond upon Thames, Surrey
1927–28	Attended St John's Wood School of Art, London; studied under Pat Millard
1929–32	Student at the Royal Academy Schools, London
1935–38	Studios in St John's Wood, London, and near Winchester, Hampshire; worked as a painter but began to experiment with sculpture
1938	Married Eileen Guthrie; moved to Uffington, Oxfordshire; later had five children
1946	Exhibition of a few works in Bristol, organized by Godfrey Pilkington (no records survive)
1947	*Sculpture in the Home*, Arts Council touring exhibition
1954	Moved to Oundle, Northamptonshire; began teaching at the local public school
1968	Solo exhibition at Fermoy Art Gallery, King's Lynn, Norfolk
1969	Solo exhibition at Somerville College, University of Cambridge, arranged by Anthony Holden
1972	*George Kennethson: Sculpture & Drawings 1952–72*, Kettle's Yard, Cambridge
1974	*A Retrospective Exhibition (1949–72): Sculptures & Drawings by George Kennethson*, University of Birmingham
1975	*George Kennethson: Sculpture*, Kettle's Yard, Cambridge
1986	*Translations from Life and Nature: Stone Carvings 1950–1985*, Peterborough Museum and Art Gallery
1988	Solo exhibition at The New Art Centre, London
1993	*George Kennethson: Retrospective*, The New Art Centre at Roche Court, Wiltshire
	Experiments and Translations, Pallant House, Chichester, West Sussex
1994	Died in Oundle, Northamptonshire
2000	*George Kennethson 1910–1994*, Wilson Stephens Fine Art, London
	George Kennethson: Retrospective, Yarrow Gallery, Oundle, Northamptonshire
2004	*George Kennethson: A Modernist Rediscovered*, Wilson Stephens Fine Art in association with Archeus Fine Art, London
1994–2004	Works exhibited at the *20/21 British Art Fair*, Royal College of Art and the Commonwealth Institute, London, and the *London Contemporary Art Fair*, Business Design Centre, Islington, London, with Wilson Stephens Fine Art

The Estate of George Kennethson is represented by Wilson Stephens Fine Art, London

INDEX

Page numbers in **bold** refer to illustrations

ACKNOWLEDGEMENTS

We wish to express our grateful thanks to all those who have contributed to this publication. In particular, we should like to thank the Mackenzie family, especially Eileen, for their invaluable help. Our thanks also go to all at Merrell.

Simon Hucker and Rosanna Wilson Stephens

First published 2004 by Merrell Publishers Limited

Head office:
42 Southwark Street
London SE1 1UN

New York office:
49 West 24th Street, 8th floor
New York, NY 10010

www.merrellpublishers.com

Publisher: Hugh Merrell
Editorial Director: Julian Honer
US Director: Joan Brookbank
Sales and Marketing Director: Emilie Amos
Sales and Marketing Executive: Emily Sanders
Managing Editor: Anthea Snow
Editor: Sam Wythe
Design Manager: Nicola Bailey
Production Manager: Michelle Draycott
Design and Production Assistant: Matt Packer

British Library Cataloguing-in-Publication Data:
Hucker, Simon
George Kennethson
1.Kennethson, George, 1910–1994 2.Sculpture – Great Britain
I.Title
730.9′2

ISBN 1 85894 277 2

Produced by Merrell Publishers Limited
Designed by Maggi Smith
Printed and bound in China

Front jacket: *Figure in Repose* (detail), *c.* 1980, private collection, England

Back jacket: Portrait of the sculptor in his studio with work in progress, 1953

Endpapers: Abstract flower design (detail), early 1940s, linocut, courtesy of Eileen Mackenzie: Kennethson and his wife, Eileen, spent a lot of time in the years after World War II developing wood and lino blocks for printing fabrics, many of which show the beginnings of the abstraction of nature into simplified forms that was to become such a feature of his sculpture.

Half title: *George Kennethson Sculpture*, linocut by the sculptor made for the catalogue of his exhibition at Kettle's Yard, Cambridge, in 1972

Frontispiece: *Boy with a Bird* (detail; see plate 28)

Page 4: The sculptor's tools against the studio wall

Pages 26–27: *Reclining Figure* (detail; see plate 29)

Photo credits

George Kennethson: figs. 1, 10, 14
Courtesy of Kettle's Yard, Cambridge: fig. 15
Matthew Mackenzie: fig. 9
Nicholas Mackenzie: figs. 7, 16
Courtesy *World of Interiors*: photographer Don Freeman (from an article about Kettle's Yard, Cambridge, *World of Interiors*, April 2000): fig. 17
Courtesy *World of Interiors*: photographer Bob Smith (from an article entitled 'Set in Stone', *World of Interiors*, October 2002): pages 4, 6, 9, 10–11

All other photographs, including the front jacket, by Miki Slingsby

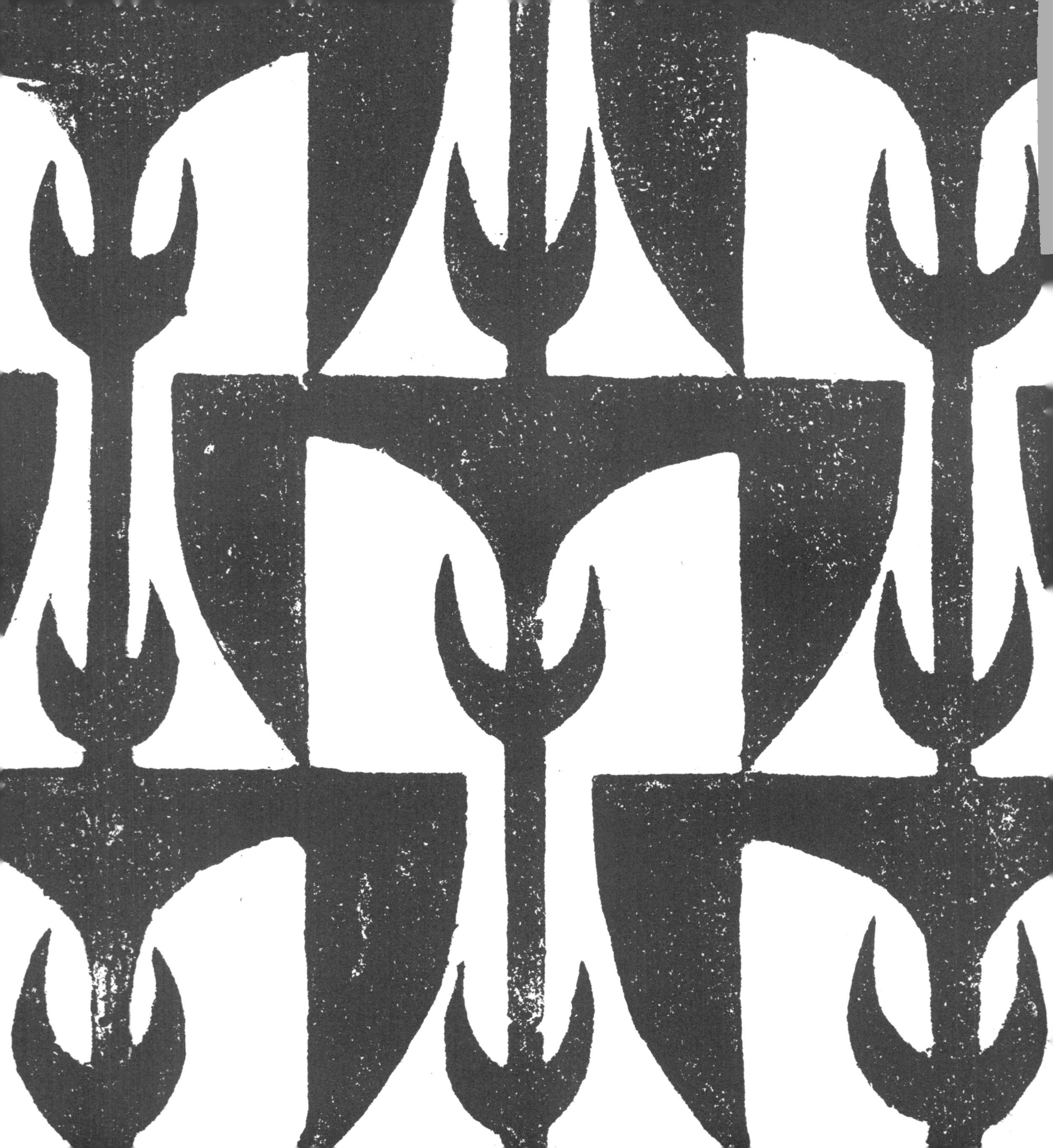